TIMOTHY PICKERING AS THE LEADER OF NEW ENGLAND FEDERALISM, 1800-1815

A Da Capo Press Reprint Series

THE AMERICAN SCENE
Comments and Commentators

GENERAL EDITOR: WALLACE D. FARNHAM
University of Illinois

TIMOTHY PICKERING AS THE LEADER OF NEW ENGLAND FEDERALISM, 1800-1815

By

HERVEY PUTNAM PRENTISS

DA CAPO PRESS • NEW YORK • 1972

Library of Congress Cataloging in Publication Data

Prentiss, Hervey Putnam, 1903-
    Timothy Pickering as the leader of New England
Federalism, 1800-1815.

    (The American scene: comments and commentators)
    Reprint of the 1934 ed., which consisted of chapters
originally presented in the author's thesis, North-
western University, 1932.
        1. Pickering, Timothy, 1745-1829. 2. Federal
Party. New England. I. Title.
E302.6.P5P7   1972   973.4'0924[B]   71-124882
ISBN 0-306-71052-8

This Da Capo Press edition of *Timothy Pickering as the Leader of
New England Federalism, 1800-1815,* is an unabridged republica-
tion of the edition reprinted in 1934 from the *Essex Institute Historical Collections* of January and April, 1933, and April, 1934. It is
reprinted by permission from a copy of that edition in the collection
of the Alderman Library, University of Virginia.

Published by Da Capo Press, Inc.
A Subsidiary of Plenum Publishing Corporation
227 West 17th Street, New York, N.Y. 10011

TIMOTHY PICKERING AS THE LEADER OF NEW ENGLAND FEDERALISM, 1800-1815

TIMOTHY PICKERING AS THE LEADER OF NEW ENGLAND FEDERALISM, 1800-1815

———

By HERVEY PUTNAM PRENTISS

Reprinted from the Essex Institute Historical Collections of January and April, 1933, and April, 1934

CONTENTS

RESIDENCE OF HON. TIMOTHY PICKERING, OFF LARCH ROW, WENHAM, DURING THE EARLY PART OF THE 19th CENTURY.

From a photograph taken in 1897.

TIMOTHY PICKERING AND THE FEDERALIST PARTY, 1801-1804.

By HERVEY PUTNAM PRENTISS.

When Timothy Pickering was dismissed from the cabinet of President Adams in May, 1800, it was with much bitterness of soul that he retired to his lands in the wilderness of northeastern Pennsylvania. His expulsion was peremptory and unceremonious to say the least,[1] but it was the result of a series of personal and political differences between the President and his Secretary of State.[2] In the cabinet, Pickering had been the official spokesman of the "Essex Junto," an inner circle of Massachusetts Federalists, who had for years dominated their state government and had led the national government to adopt the policies of a mercantile aristocracy.[3] Thus, his dismissal was one of the elements in the decline of the national influence of Massachusetts Federalism. When Jefferson came

[1] C. F. Adams, *The Life and Works of John Adams* (10 vols., Boston, 1850-56), IX, 53-56.

[2] H. J. Ford, "Timothy Pickering" in S. F. Bemis (ed.), *American Secretaries of State and Their Diplomacy* (New York, 1927), vol. II, is the best account of Pickering's work in the State Department and of his long conflict with Adams over American policy toward England and France. The published *Correspondence* (Boston, 1823) of John Adams and William Cunningham and Pickering's *Review* (Salem, 1824) of that work contain ample evidence of the personal feud between them.

[3] Pickering's correspondence with Fisher Ames, George Cabot, and Stephen Higginson is sufficient proof of his relation to the "Junto." Most of these letters are preserved in the Pickering MSS. at the Massachusetts Historical Society and many of them are printed in Seth Ames, *Works of Fisher Ames* (2 vols., Boston, 1854), "The letters of Stephen Higginson" in the *Am. Hist. Assoc. Report* (1896, vol. I), and H. C. Lodge, *Life and Letters of George Cabot* (Boston, 1877).

into power in 1801, the destruction of that influence was practically complete, for the Republicanism then sweeping the country had little use for the political ideals of the commercial class.

In retiring to Pennsylvania, it was Pickering's purpose to withdraw permanently from politics and to devote his attention to the development of some tracts of land which he had owned for several years. His Massachusetts friends uniformly attempted to dissuade him from this course and they urged him to return to his native state where their influence could secure him a public office.[4] He answered that they exaggerated the difficulties and hardships of living in the wilderness. He was willing to accept a public office in the national government, but he recognized that it would be impossible for him to hold one under Jefferson. As for a seat on the Massachusetts Supreme Court, he could not accept it as it would enable him only to "starve with decency."[5] He preferred to proceed with his land projects in the hope that they would enable him to acquire a moderate fortune. Even when two of his friends, Timothy Williams and Samuel Putnam, made a special trip to Philadelphia to urge him to return to Massachusetts, he steadfastly refused to abandon his plans.[6]

During the summer of 1800, he was full of schemes for the development of his property, most of which lay along the upper Susquehanna near the New York line. He proposed to survey it and subdivide it into one hundred acre tracts which he would offer for sale. In order to attract settlers and to increase the value of the land, he planned to build a saw-mill and a grist-mill.[7] In addition he suggested to some of his Philadelphia friends who

[4] Pickering MSS., Letters from Benjamin Goodhue, May 19; Theodore Lyman, May 26; Christopher Gore, May 27; Samuel P. Gardner, June 15, 1800. Lodge, *Cabot*, 272-73, Cabot to Pickering, May 26, 1800.

[5] Ibid., Pickering to Benjamin Goodhue, May 31; to Christopher Gore, June 9; to Samuel P. Gardner, June 21, 1800.

[6] Octavius Pickering and Charles W. Upham, *Life of Timothy Pickering* (4 vols., Boston, 1867-73), IV, 5-7. Williams was a Boston merchant and a nephew of Pickering, while Putnam was a Salem lawyer who had married Pickering's niece.

[7] Pickering MSS., Pickering to Tench Coxe and Samuel Hodgdon, June 25, 1800.

owned land in the vicinity of his own that they co-operate with him in the building of roads and permit him to act as their agent in the survey and sale of their property.[8] Unfortunately he lacked the capital required for such work and had to apply to his old friends in Massachusetts for loans. Although they disapproved of his plans, they came to his aid with the necessary funds.[9] Thus provided with money, he left his family at Easton, Pennsylvania, and set out for the wilderness where he remained until early winter.[10]

Returning to Easton in December, he decided to make a visit to his old home in Salem, possibly with the idea that he might be able to sell some of his lands there. While he was in Salem, his friends naturally tried again to get him to give up his land schemes and to return to Massachusetts to live. They soon learned that he could not easily be persuaded to surrender his project. Consequently, a number of prominent men, interested in his welfare and, incidentally, in securing his political services, banded together to purchase his property. As their agent, Samuel Putnam called on him to ask at what price he would dispose of his holdings. In reply, Pickering gave Putnam a written description of his lands and stated the cash prices for which he would be willing to sell them. Altogether there were about 24,000 acres which he valued at $33,000.[11] The interested men quickly agreed to his terms. Thirty-four of them subscribed 250 shares at $100 a share to purchase a three-quarter interest in the property while Pickering retained the rest.[12] At the same time he was appointed agent for the group and authorized to sell the lands on commission whenever an

8 Pickering MSS., Pickering to Tench Coxe and Samuel Hodgdon, June 25, 1800.

9 Pickering and Upham, *Pickering*, IV, 13-14.

10 *Ibid.*, 14-20.

11 Pickering and Upham, *Pickering*, IV, 26-27, Pickering to Putnam, Feb. 11, 1801. The lands described in this document are: (1) twenty-five tracts containing between 10,000 and 11,000 acres located on Snake Creek which flows into the Susquehanna a few miles below Great Bend; (2) about 4,000 acres on Little Sugar Creek; and (3) about 9,000 acres in western Pennsylvania about forty miles east of the Alleghany River and near the road from Philadelphia to Presqu' Isle (Erie, Pa.).

12 *Ibid.*, 28-29, Pickering to Eben Parsons et al, April 1, 1801.

opportunity should present itself.[13] This transaction enabled him to clear himself of debt and return to Massachusetts with a cash balance of $14,000.[14] With this sum he could become financially independent and purchase a small farm in Essex County.

In November, 1801, Timothy Pickering brought his family to Salem where they were able to celebrate Thanksgiving among their relatives and friends. Early in the next year they moved to a small farm in Danvers which they had leased.[15] This place turned out to be unsatisfactory and two years later they moved to another rented farm in Upper Beverly. As it was Pickering's desire to purchase a good farm with a large house, he kept this only until he could find a place that met his requirements. Finally he obtained one in Wenham and purchased it, moving there in 1806.[16] This remained his home for many years.

The character of the arrangement which made possible Pickering's return to Massachusetts is obvious. The purchasers of his lands had no real desire for the property and did not expect to turn it to account as all of them were engaged in more profitable pursuits. Their real interest lay in securing his return with the expectation that it would lead to his re-entry into political life where he could perform important services for the Federalist party. Nearly all the purchasers were well-to-do Federalist merchants and lawyers of Boston and Salem. Prominent among them were two members of the "Essex Junto," George Cabot and Stephen Higginson.[17] They

[13] Pickering MSS., Eben Parsons to Pickering, Apr. 1, 1801.
[14] Pickering and Upham, *Pickering*, IV, 28.
[15] *Ibid.*, 42-43.
[16] *Ibid.*, 99.
[17] Pickering and Upham, *Pickering*, IV, 28-29, Pickering to Eben Parsons et al, Apr. 1, 1801, gives the names of all the subscribers. Some others of note were Samuel Blanchard of Wenham, an ardent Federalist and a friend of Pickering; Thomas Handasyd Perkins, a wealthy Boston merchant and later a member of the Hartford Convention; Theodore Lyman, a Boston merchant; Benjamin Pickman, a leading Federalist merchant of Salem; James Lloyd, Jr., later Pickering's colleague in the Senate; William Prescott, another member of the Hartford Convention; Israel Thorndike, Beverly's leading merchant; John Lowell, Jr., the great pamphleteer of the Federalists; and William Gray, reputed to be the richest merchant of the time.

were men who recognized the relation between commerce and politics. In Pickering they saw a man whose devotion to the principles of Federalism was complete and who fully identified the national interest with the interests of maritime commerce. To return him to political life might amply repay all that they had spent to bring him back to Massachusetts. That this was their purpose became clear enough when he was appointed Chief Justice of the Court of Common Pleas for Essex County in 1802[18] and later in the same year became a candidate for Congress. The Republicans, of course, suspected the reason for his return and they openly declared:

"He was only obliged to become an inhabitant of Essex, to be set up as a candidate for Congress, to lose his livelihood by being made a Chief Justice of the Court of Common Pleas, and in fine to persist in the accomplishment of Hamilton's old scheme of MONARCHY!!!"[19]

On September 21 it was announced that the Honorable Nathan Read, then the Representative from the Essex South District, would not stand for re-election[20] and three days later Pickering was proposed as the Federalist candidate for that office.[21] The Republicans countered shortly with the nomination of Captain Jacob Crowninshield, a member of a distinguished family of Salem merchants.[22] Up to this time Essex County had always been overwhelmingly Federalist,[23] but now there were indications that not even this stronghold of Federalism would be able to resist the growing popularity of Jefferson's Republican party. It was, perhaps, a recognition of this condition that led the Federalists to nominate the ex-Secretary of State in the hope that the prestige of his name could halt the rising tide of Republicanism.

The campaign was one of violence, characterized by the

[18] Pickering and Upham, *Pickering*, IV, 43.
[19] *Essex Register*, Oct. 25, 1802.
[20] *Salem Gazette*, Sept. 21, 1802.
[21] *Ibid.*, Sept. 24, 1802.
[22] *Essex Register*, Oct. 11, 1802.
[23] W. W. Story, *Life of Joseph Story* (2 vols., Boston, 1851), I, 95. When Story began his law practice in 1801, he found that all positions of importance in the county were held by Federalists and that the prejudice against Republicans was so strong that he had great difficulty in securing clients.

flow of abusive language from the organs of both parties. The leading Federalist paper was the *Salem Gazette* and it was conducted with the very evident aim of consciously serving the interests of the most "respectable" people of the community. The Republicans were represented by the *Essex Register* which was as ardent in its attacks on Federalism as the *Gazette* was in its defence.[24]   Foremost among the supporters of the *Register* and Republicanism was a liberal minister, the Reverend William Bentley, whose understanding of political problems was quite as acute as his handling of theological questions. He was the most cultured man in Salem and his many interests and activities were worthy of a follower of the versatile Jefferson.   His politics was as liberal as his religion and the strength of democracy among the upper classes of Salem was attributable in part to his influence, for among his parishioners were many sea-captains and merchants, including the prominent Crowninshield family.   He was a frequent contributor to the *Register,* usually preparing the excellent summary of foreign news that appeared in its pages.   Many of its political editorials were ascribed to him by the Federalists, though it is doubtful that he wrote them.   For Pickering he had only the greatest contempt, referring to him in his *Diary* as

"that pest of Society . . . who has returned to curse the neighborhood, which has already been abused by his controversies and contraventions."[25]

As Salem's chief interest lay in commerce and as it was the most important town of the district, the major efforts of the parties were designed to capture the votes of its seafaring people.   Electioneering articles signed by "Tom Steadybreeze," "Bill Boltrope," and "Bill Bobstay" appeared in the newspapers, picturing Pickering either as an enemy to sailors' rights or as a protector of them, according to the politics of the writer.   "Bill Boltrope" declared for Pickering and said:

[24] Harriet S. Tapley, *Salem Imprints, 1768-1825* (Salem, 1927), contains an excellent account of these newspapers and their political controversies.

[25] Reverend William Bentley, *Diary* (4 vols., Salem, 1905-14), II, 457-58.

". . . though the jacobins make such a hurly-burly about liberty and equality, I have never found they treated those that work for them so well as the federalists, except now and then of a town meeting day when they are mighty palavering. . . . I never could like these all-talk-and-no-cider folks, they put me so much in mind of Virginia people, that preach about liberty, and use their poor black devils like so many dogs. It seems to me that nothing good ever came out of Virginia except Washington and tobacco."[26]

To this sally the *Register* replied:

" 'Bill Boltrope' will deserve to have a rope under his bill if he votes for a man who preferred the word of honor of an Englishman to the solemn oath of his own Countrymen—more especially when he can bestow his suffrage on a Gentleman who has risked his life in defence of American-Seamen—and who is not a Pickaroon."[27]

In this mudslinging campaign, the Republicans outdid their rivals. As Pickering had had a much longer political career than Crowninshield, they had an opportunity to dig up all the questionable acts of his public life, including his late arrival at "Concord Fight."[28] He was attacked as a "known and open reviler of Washington and Adams,"[29] as an opponent of peace with France, an advocate of the Alien and Sedition Acts, a supporter of internal revenue taxes and the increase of the public debt, and a believer in monarchy.[30] But the crowning effort of all was the allegation that Robert Liston, the British minister, had distributed $500,000 among British partisans in the United States, among whom Pickering was conspicuous. Concerning this the *Register* asked,

". . . Can you entirely banish from your breast, the idea that our ex-Secretary might receive from his dear friend and intimate companion some little token, some small gratuity, for all his zealous efforts against liberty and her sons, for all his attachments to the interests of England, . . . ?"[31]

26 *Salem Gazette*, Oct. 12, 1802.
27 *Essex Register*, Oct. 14, 1802.
28 *Ibid.*
29 *Ibid.*, Oct. 4, 1802.
30 *Essex Register*, Oct. 14, 1802.
31 *Ibid.*, Oct. 28, 1802.

The *Gazette* issued blanket denials of every charge against Pickering and declared that

"Aspersion and vile detraction are instruments by which pure patriotism and sound principles were driven from the seats of honor to make room for hypocritical pretensions and rotten-hearted republicanism."[32]

The *Register's* charge of Pickering's having received a British pension came too late in the campaign to be given an adequate answer and after the election the Federalists resorted to a libel suit against Carlton, the editor.[33]   But the *Gazette* was not averse to the use of strong language and declared that Crowninshield was "like a piece of old rope, the more you try to splice it, the worse it grows."[34]

The election itself was a riotous affair and the defeated Federalists indulged themselves freely in charges of fraud that could not be proved.   Crowninshield was elected by a vote of 1,400 to 1,293.   His success rested entirely on his ability to carry the seaport towns of Salem, Marblehead, and Gloucester.   All of the others returned majorities for Pickering.[35]   Apparently the appeal to the sailors had worked and the Federalists had been discredited among the lower classes of the seaports.[36]   The Federalists were much disappointed in the result, yet the *Gazette* maintained that

"The vote of Monday was highly honorable to Mr. Pickering, though it did not secure his election.   He had the support of the property, respectability and ancient inhabitants of this district."[37]

The Republicans, of course, were jubilant.   When it was learned that the election throughout the nation had been generally favorable, the *Register* announced under the heading of "Ship News Extra":

[32] *Salem Gazette*, Oct. 8, 1802.
[33] *Ibid.*, Nov. 19, 1802.
[34] *Ibid.*, Oct. 8, 1802.
[35] *Ibid.*, Nov. 2, 1802.
[36] Later elections show a similar division with the lower classes of the large towns supporting the Republicans, while the Federalists relied heavily on the country towns in Essex County. An important factor in the vote of the rural districts was the presence of many retired sea-captains and other men of small property who were naturally attracted to Federalism.
[37] *Salem Gazette*, Nov. 5, 1802.

"We are happy to hear that the fast sailing and sound ship *Republican Constitutionalist,* on the 1st inst. passed the old piratical ship *Essex Junto* under jury masts, and water logged with no persons on board—the Officers and crew, with the *Rats,* having deserted her just in season to save their bacon. 'Stormy weather,' say the Officers and crew, prevented their saving the *Old Hulk.* Her tender, the *Pickaroon,* had been previously chased ashore on *Cape Despair* by the Republican 'bomb ketch.' We are told, that the *Essex Junto* belonged to the House of *Hamilton, Pinckney, Pickering,* & Co. She was not insured as she was not seaworthy."[38]

Feeling keenly the result of an election which had rejected an ex-Secretary of State, Pickering found it necessary to vent his wrath on someone and the subject of his choice was Carlton, the editor of the *Register,* against whom he instituted libel proceedings.[39] The suit was denounced by the Republicans as "PERSECUTION,"[40] but it was impossible for them to prove that Pickering had received money from Liston as Carlton had charged during the campaign. In the end, the editor was convicted and sentenced to pay a fine of $100 and costs, spend two months in jail, and give a bond of $800 to keep the peace for two years.[41]

Having failed to place their favorite in the House of Representatives after they had spent $25,000 to bring him back to Massachusetts, the arch-Federalist faction of the state now laid their plans to get him into the Senate and thus provide themselves with a spokesman at Washington. Hearing a rumor of this plan, the *Essex Register* published a lampoon entitled "The Humble Petition of the Essex Junto, to the Hon. Jona. Mason and Hon. Dwight Foster, Senators of the U. States for Massachusetts," which called on the above named Senators to resign in order that "the political giant, Timothy," might be sent to the Senate to represent the Junto.[42] As Mason's term

38 *Essex Register,* Nov. 22, 1802. Another notable Republican success of the same election was the victory of Dr. William Eustis over John Quincy Adams.
39 Bentley, *Diary,* II, 457.
40 *Essex Register,* Nov. 18, 1802.
41 Tapley, *Salem Imprints,* 172.
42 *Essex Register,* Dec. 6, 1802.

was to expire on March 3, 1803, his resignation was not necessary and the way was cleared for the Essex men to propose Pickering's name to the Massachusetts legislature. At the same time Fisher Ames and John Quincy Adams were mentioned as candidates. Ames refused to be named, but Adams was not at all averse to being advanced to the national Congress.

The Federalist party was then in complete control of the state government, possessing clear majorities in both houses of the legislature, but the party itself was sharply divided on the question of electing a Senator. The majority favored Adams, but the "Junto" insisted on Pickering. At length a compromise was reached, for it appeared that two Senators would be chosen that year, as Foster was planning to resign his seat. This situation made possible the election of both men. But even then there was difficulty, for the "Junto" wished to have Pickering elected for the six year term, with Adams receiving the remaining two years of Foster's term. Obviously this created complications when Adams was clearly the more popular of the two, even in Massachusetts.[43]

The only agreement that could be reached by a Federalist caucus was to place both names in nomination and to support Pickering on the first two ballots. Then, if no candidate had a majority, the members of the caucus and their friends would vote for Adams on the third ballot. It happened that Pickering could not get a majority, but the adherents of the "Junto" were unwilling to abandon him and a third ballot was taken without resulting in a choice. Finally, on the fourth attempt, all but six of the Federalists voted for Adams and a majority was secured. This hesitation to support him aroused Adams' ire and he blamed John Lowell and Harrison Gray Otis for the delay in his election.[44] Pickering's anger at the result can only be imagined. To be defeated by the son of the man who had driven him from office less than three years earlier was a severe blow and must certainly have increased his resentment against the Adams family. All

[43] C. F. Adams (ed.), *Memoirs of John Quincy Adams* (12 vols., Philadelphia, 1874-77), I, 256.
[44] *Ibid.*, 257-59.

that was left for him was to take the unexpired term of
Dwight Foster and to this he was duly chosen early in
March, 1803.[45]

When Pickering entered the Senate in the fall, the fortunes of Federalism were at a low ebb. Little by little
the party was being shorn of its power as its representation in Congress dwindled and Federalist office-holders
were being gradually replaced by the adherents of Jefferson. Especially bitter at this turn of events were the
high Federalists of New England against whom in par-
ticular Jefferson aimed his "regeneracy of offices."[46] In
this condition, their state of mind was well expressed by
Fisher Ames when he wrote,

". . . democracy is only the isthmus of a middle state:
it is nothing of itself. Like death it is only the dismal
passport to a more dismal hereafter. Such is our state."[47]

Thus reduced to a weak minority in the national government, many of the Federalists were ready for extreme
measures and were prepared to offer the most intransi-
geant opposition to the Jeffersonian policies. To repre-
sent them in this opposition, the "Junto" could scarcely
have chosen a more devoted adherent of their political philosophy or a more sincere hater of everything tinged with
Jeffersonianism than Timothy Pickering. He entered
the Senate in October prepared to admit no compromise
with his political enemies.[48]

[45] *Salem Gazette*, Mar. 4, 1803.

[46] Thomas Jefferson, *Works* (P. L. Ford, ed., 12 vols., New
York, 1904-05), VIII, 66-67, Jefferson to Levi Lincoln, July 11,
1801. ". . . We must strip of all the means of influence the
Essex Junto, and their associate monocrats in every part of
the Union."

[47] Ames, *Works*, I, 322-27, Ames to Christopher Gore, Oct. 3,
1803.

[48] His hatred of Jefferson is well illustrated by a letter to
Rufus Putnam (Dec. 6, 1803, Pickering MSS.). Offering his
regrets at Putnam's removal from the office of surveyor-general,
Pickering said: "Alas! mistaken soldier! You find, after the
lapse of only twenty years, that liberty is the right of adopting the political opinions of our present chief ruler, & independence, the privilege of bowing obsequiously to his will.
This, however, was a lesson which you, my friend, were incapable of learning. Firm in virtue, and inviolably attached to
the correct principles of Washington, you could not descend to
the degrading level of *modern patriotism*, under which are
masqued inordinate ambition, and every base and selfish passion."

However, the ability of the Federalists to offer an effective opposition to Jefferson was seriously impaired by their own internal divisions.   The schism of 1800 had not been healed and the party was still split between the supporters of Hamilton and the "Junto" and the more moderate faction which had followed Adams.   Jefferson was fully conscious of this state of affairs and hoped to profit from it by attracting the moderates to the support of Republicanism while he conducted a vigorous campaign against the "Essexmen."   Federalists recognized the dangers in this situation, but the "Junto," instead of trying to heal the breach in the party, regarded the moderates as only a little less obnoxious than the Jeffersonians themselves and thus lost all possibility of securing their votes.   Outstanding among the moderate Federalists, who were relatively weak in the number of their leaders, was John Quincy Adams, whom the "Junto" regarded with great suspicion.   Concerning him, Higginson wrote to Pickering:

"You know your colleague, his character, feeling and views.   It is believed that he will be more crooked than ever, soured by the loss of property in the hands of Bird & Co. who have failed, & by the shade in which he and his father are inclosed.   some think he will try to recover their lost ground, by attempting to build up a party of moderate independent men.   This was the last resort of his father, but it did not and can[not] succeed, though all the timid wavering and temporizing of both Federalists and Jacobins should be invited to join.   others think he will endeavor to conciliate the ruling party & get again into office under their patronage; but this is a game he cannot play well enough to succeed."[49]

Such factional hostility as this augured ill for the success of the party and it was to prove an insuperable handicap in the fight against Jefferson.

By all odds the most significant problem facing the country when Congress assembled in 1803 was the Louisiana question.   When the purchase of the territory was first announced, it was hailed with delight, even in the

[49] Pickering MSS., Higginson to Pickering, Oct. 12, 1803.

strongholds of Federalism.[50]   But when the terms of the
treaty were learned, Federalists began to complain that
the purchase price was too great and that the acquisition
of the new territory might lead to a considerable emigra-
tion from the eastern states.[51]   Others declared that the
Republican party's French sympathies were at the bottom
of the transaction and that the United States, in buying
Louisiana, was aiding "the world's worst foe at a moment
when its best friends are entitled to every help."[52]

The really significant cause of popular Federalist hostility, however, lay in the fact that the Louisiana Purchase was, in part, a western measure designed to favor
the agricultural interests of the frontier regions and
to secure the support of the West for the Republican
party.   It seemed that the new acquisition would inevitably injure the interests of commerce, Federalism, and
the northeastern states.   In that sense, it was a sectional
measure and aroused sectional resentment.   The *Salem
Gazette* voiced this opinion when it exclaimed,

"Fifteen Millions of Dollars for Louisiana! This is a
bargain that does not meet with unqualified approval in the
public papers. . . . Who is to pay the money? By the
present system of revenue, certainly not those directly bene-
fitted by the purchase. The money will be raised, not on
the gilt carriages of Virginians, or on the whiskey of Kentucky and Tennessee; but on the opulence of the middle, the
industry and enterprise of the northern states."[53]

Furthermore, the clause of the treaty which provided for
the incorporation of Louisiana into the Union threatened
to destroy the New England commercial interests as a
national political force, for new states west of the Mississippi were sure to become allies of the South and the old
West. The execution of this clause, said the *Newburyport Herald,* would bring about a "Revolution in our country" involving "a complete alteration in its political pow-

[50] The *Newburyport Herald* (July 1, 1803), for example, wrote:
"This province will prove a valuable acquisition to our growing
empire. . . . We pleasurably yield a tribute of praise for one
meritorious transaction of the present administration."
[51] *Newburyport Herald,* Aug. 6, 1803.
[52] *Columbian Centinel,* July 23, Aug. 13, 1803.
[53] Aug. 16, 1803.

ers and influences."[54] In pursuing this line of attack,
Federalist papers argued that the treaty was unconstitutional because the Constitution did not authorize the buying of territory[55] and because the Purchase would upset
the sectional balance of power on which the existence of
the Union was based.[56] In effect, it was believed that
the addition of Louisiana practically dissolved the Union
by this destruction of the sectional balance.[57]

Such opinions voiced in the public prints were substantially the same as those held by the party leaders.
Christopher Gore, for example, believed that as a result
of the Purchase, the end of the Union was near.

"Wise men." he wrote, "should turn their thoughts to
what will be the next chapter in our every varying systems;
for I really believe that the present is nearly read through.
a few, but very few verses remain; and those, like some of
the old testament ones, full of hard names."[58]

Stephen Higginson told Pickering that the measure was
an "essential part" of a "deliberate plan" of the Virginians "to govern and depress New England" and urged
him and his Federalist colleagues to oppose the Republicans "with vigor and firmness."[59]

In October, while the Federalist papers were denouncing the treaty, Congress assembled at Washington and
turned first to deal with the Louisiana question. The
Federalists had no chance to defeat the treaty and the
measures associated with it as the Republicans outnumbered them in both houses of Congress. The Senate
quickly voted, without much discussion, to ratify the
treaty,[60] but when a bill to approve a stock issue of
$11,250,000 to cover the payments to France came before
it, the Federalist opposition opened its attack on the
administration. This attack was made on the same line

[54] Aug. 9, 1803.
[55] *Salem Gazette*, Sept. 23, 1803.
[56] *Ibid.*, Nov. 15, 1803.
[57] *Salem Gazette*, Nov. 15, 1803.
[58] C. R. King, *Life and Correspondence of Rufus King* (6 vols.,
New York, 1894-1900). IV, 319-20, Gore to King, Nov. 1, 1803.
[59] *Am. Hist. Assoc. Report* (1896), I, 737, Higginson to Pickering, Nov. 22, 1803.
[60] *Annals of Congress.* Eighth Congress, first session, 308.
Seven Federalists, including Pickering, voted in the negative.

that the Federalists in the House had taken a week earlier
in the debate on a bill enabling the President to take possession of Louisiana.[61] The basis of this opposition as
brought out in the debates in the House of Representatives
was well summarized by Manasseh Cutler, the Federalist
Representative from the Essex North District when he
wrote:

"I am among ye number opposed—for I am clearly of
opinion that ye Treaty is unconstitutional—that ye sum
given is too much—& that in its operation, it will be inju-
rious to ye interests, & particularly the commerce of ye
Eastern States. There is no evidence that Spain has con-
cented to this treaty, but strong suspicion that ye Spanish
Government is opposed to ye purchase. It may eventually
involve us in war with Spain."[62]

It was in pursuance of this same line of argument that
the Senate Federalists attacked the administration's bill
to create the $11,250,000 stock issue. Inasmuch as the
treaty had already been ratified and both houses had overwhelmingly voted a bill enabling the President to take
possession of Louisiana, this opposition could not have
hoped to defeat the bill; its main purpose must have been
to give further publicity to the Federalist cause, hoping
thereby to build up a strong public opinion in the northern
states to support the party leaders in later projects. The
major speeches against the bill were delivered by Pickering and Uriah Tracy, a Connecticut Senator, whose Federalism and sectional feeling were as ardent as his colleague's. The administration speakers had declared that
the passage of the bill was obligatory, for the treaty had
been duly ratified and had thus become part of the law
of the land. From this opinion Pickering dissented, believing that a treaty, to be binding, must not violate the
Constitution as this one certainly did. There was no
question, he thought, of the right of the government to
acquire territory by purchase or conquest and to govern
it as a dependent province, but it had no constitutional

61 Henry Adams, *History of the United States during the ad-
ministrations of Thomas Jefferson and James Madison* (9 vols.,
New York, 1889-91), II, 95-104.
62 *Essex Inst. Hist. Coll.*, XXXIX, 321, Cutler to Francis Low,
Oct. 26, 1803.

right to incorporate such territory into the Union. He could not accept the clause authorizing Congress to admit new states as a justification for this provision of the treaty, for he declared that the Constitution had contemplated only the creation of new states out of the original territory of the nation and not the incorporation of a foreign country into the Union. He believed, quite correctly, that the administration thought that this article was unconstitutional and that it would require a constitutional amendment.[63] However, he disagreed with Jefferson's idea that a simple amendment was sufficient; in this case he believed that the consent of each state was necessary, just as a commercial house in admitting a new partner required the consent of all of its members. Such consent, he was free to declare, could never be obtained.[64]

Outside of its unconstitutional character, the cession was open to other objections, said the New England leader. He believed that the title of France to Louisiana was deficient and that Spain could reasonably object to the transfer. In that case, war between the United States and Spain would almost surely be the result and, inasmuch as France was the ally of Spain, that nation, as soon as the war with Great Britain was off her hands, would join the Spaniards in trying to wrest the territory from the United States. In fact, he was convinced that France had negotiated the treaty with this end in view, for he looked upon her as the most perfidious of nations. Furthermore, the boundaries of Louisiana were very obscurely defined in the treaty and this, too, he believed, was purposely intended to provoke later difficulties. Altogether, he could see nothing in the cession but the prospect of future trouble for the United States,[65]

Tracy likewise thought the treaty unconstitutional, but he rested his arguments less on the literal breach of the

[63] Cf. Jefferson's opinion: "I do not believe it was meant that Congress might receive England, Ireland, Holland, etc., into it, . . . I had rather ask an enlargement of power from the nation, where it is found necessary, than to assume it by a construction which would make our powers boundless." *Works*, IV, 505, Jefferson to W. C. Nicholas, Sept. 7, 1803.

[64] *Annals*, 8th, 1st, 44-47.

[65] *Annals*, 8th, 1st, 44-47.

Constitution than on what he conceived to be a violation of the principle of the Union.

"The principle of admission, in the case of Louisiana," he said, "is the same as if it contained ten millions of inhabitants; and the principles of these people are probably as hostile to our government, in the true construction, as they can be, and the relative strength which this admission gives to a Southern and Western interest, is contradictory to the principles of our original Union, as any can be, however strongly stated."

Inevitably, he thought, it would mean the destruction of the balance of sectional interests which the Constitution was calculated to maintain. Like Pickering, he believed that the consent of the individual states was necessary to carry out the treaty and he declared:

". . . this universal consent I am positive can never be obtained to such a pernicious measure as the admission of Louisiana, of a world, and such a world, into our Union. This would be absorbing the Northern States, and rendering them insignificant in the Union, as they ought to be, if, by their own consent, the measure should be adopted."[66]

Some of the supporters of the administration found the arguments of the New Englanders embarrassing, for at the time of the Alien and Sedition Acts a few years earlier, they had themselves championed a constitutional theory not unlike that of Pickering and Tracy, but there were others, especially from the West, who felt none of that embarrassment. One of them, Senator Breckinridge of Kentucky, declared that the right of the President and Congress to acquire territory in the name of the nation was unlimited. In answer to the argument that the cession endangered the existence of the Union, he threatened the secession of the West if the measure were not passed.[67]

Thus did the leaders of sectional political opinion proclaim their extreme views. Midway between them stood John Quincy Adams whose moderation was proof enough that extremists like Pickering and Tracy were far from having the united support of their own section and their own party. Like them, he had constitutional objections to

[66] *Annals*, 8th, 1st, 53-58.
[67] *Ibid.*, 58-65.

the treaty, but unlike them he believed that a simple constitutional amendment was the proper solution of the problem, which was precisely the view held by Jefferson. In further contrast to the high Federalists, Adams approved the Purchase as a measure of public policy and he hoped that the discussion would end "in our full, undisturbed and undisputed possession of the ceded territory."[68]

The opposition of the Federalists was, however, doomed to end in defeat. When the bill was put to a vote, it was passed, twenty-six to five. Only Hillhouse of Connecticut and Wells and White of Delaware voted with Pickering and Tracy against it.[69] Although the New Hampshire Senators, Plumer and Olcott, had opposed the ratification of the treaty, believing that the cession would dwarf the interests of New England and lead to its separation from the Union,[70] they now voted with the majority because they believed that ratification made obligatory the passage of the bills to carry out the treaty.[71]

Inasmuch as the Louisiana question was the most important cause of the plans for secession which occupied so large a place in the minds of Pickering and his friends shortly after this, it is worthwhile to inquire whether failure to block the treaty and the measures associated with it produced that reaction in them immediately. Apparently it did not. In spite of Pickering's bitter opposition to the Louisiana bill, he preferred to see that region under the control of the United States rather than of France. Nearly three weeks after the Senate debate of November third he wrote to Caleb Strong that the cession would be "productive of fewer evils than Louisiana in the hands of France." He predicted that eventually Louisiana would support a great population which would unite with the people between the Alleghenies and the Mississippi and separate from the eastern states.

"This event, however, is remote," he said. "The naviga-

[68] *Annals*, 8th, 1st, 65-68.
[69] *Ibid.*, 73.
[70] W. Plumer, *Life of William Plumer* (Boston, 1856), 285.
[71] E. S. Brown, ed., *William Plumer's memorandum of proceedings in the United States Senate, 1803-07* (Univ. of Mich. Pub.: History and Political Science, vol. V, New York, 1923), 30-32.

tion of the Atlantic States will be essential to the dwellers in the Mississippi regions. This commercial intercourse will be mutually beneficial: and while they will find their advantage in it, the Atlantic States may control and effectually regulate the navigation and commerce of those regions."

On the other hand, if France were to continue in possession of Louisiana, he predicted that French control of the river would "at no distant time" force the Americans east of the Mississippi to secede and join the French. "Thus," he said, "our Union would be severed and we would lose control of the commerce of the Mississippi valley."[72]

Although other Federalist leaders approved of the stand which Pickering had taken in Congress, they, too, were unwilling to carry their opposition further at this time. Richard Peters wrote that if he had been in Congress, he would have voted for the treaty, but with a protest against all the things which were wrong in it.[73] Governor Strong congratulated the Senator on opposing the cession, as he believed that any enlargement of the Union must lead to dissolution, but he advocated no further steps of opposition.[74] Higginson viewed the cession with alarm as he saw the Republicans gaining strength in every part of the nation, but he contented himself with urging a firm and united opposition to administration measures.[75] Cabot reported that he was greatly pleased with Pickering's speech, although he bewailed the declining influence of Federalism and declared that he was "mortified" at John Quincy Adams' support of the administration.[76] Rufus King had the same constitutional objections to the treaty as Pickering. He, too, feared the increase in strength which the Republicans would gain and he suggested that this might be partially offset by an amendment to destroy the slave representation enjoyed by the South.[77]

Following the ratification of the Louisiana Treaty and

[72] Pickering MSS., Pickering to Strong, Nov. 5, 1803.
[73] *Ibid.*, Peters to Pickering, Nov. 22, 1803.
[74] *Ibid.*, Strong to Pickering, Nov. 7, 1803.
[75] *Am. Hist. Assoc. Report* (1896), I, 837, Higginson to Pickering, Nov. 22, 1803.
[76] Lodge, *Cabot*, 333.
[77] King, *Life and Correspondence of Rufus King*, IV, 324.

the adoption of measures to complete the cession, the administration forces turned to the consideration of other policies which seriously irritated and disturbed the New England Federalists.   The most important of these questions were the Twelfth Amendment, the impeachment of the judges, and bills for the organization and government of Louisiana.   In each case, the Republicans were victorious and, in consequence, the bitterness of the Federalists increased.

In the debate on the amendment, Pickering and Tracy again led the opposition.   Pickering denied that its real purpose was to prevent a recurrence of the situation of 1800 as its sponsors had claimed, and asserted that their real intention was to make more complete the rule of the dominant section and the majority party.   The existing constitutional provision for the choice of the executive, he said, had been drawn up as an adjustment of the balance of power among the states and any alteration would be sure to destroy that balance.[78]   Hillhouse, Tracy, and White presented similar arguments and emphasized the potential danger of the amendment to the rights of the small states.[79]   But all their opposition was unavailing and the Senate adopted the amendment by a party vote.[80] On this occasion John Quincy Adams joined the other New Englanders in voting against the measure, although he favored the principle of naming the President and Vice-President separately.   His objection was to the clause which provided for the submission of the names of the three leading candidates to the House of Representatives in case no candidate should receive a majority in the electoral college and he proposed an amendment to substitute "five" for "three."   In this proposal all the New England Senators but Pickering supported him.[81] The antipathy between the two men was so great that they could scarcely agree on any policy.[82]

Failing to halt the amendment in Congress, Pickering

[78] *Annals*, 8th, 1st, 195-99.
[79] *Ibid.*, 89-90, 139-51.
[80] *Ibid*, 209.
[81] *Ibid.*, 124; Pickering MSS., Pickering to Timothy Williams, Jan. 3, 1804; to Stephen Higginson, Jan. 6, 1804.
[82] Adams, *Memoirs of J. Q. Adams*, I, 288.

turned to the states in a futile attempt to defeat ratification. To this end he distributed among his influential friends copies of his own and Tracy's speeches as he urged them to prevent ratification.[83] Though his friends were prompt to thank him and to express their approval of his stand,[84] nothing was accomplished.

The impeachment of the judges was regarded as particularly objectionable and was correctly interpreted as a means of depriving the Federalists of their last stronghold in the government. When the House voted to begin its inquiry into the conduct of Chase and Peters, Pickering told Higginson,

"I further understand, that it is the intention of the party to impeach every judge, who, in his charges to Grand-Juries, has given a political opinion."[85]

To Theodore Lyman he reported that the object of the administration was to remove the Federalist judges who constituted the last obstacle in the way of Republican domination. The Republicans aimed, he said, at making Congress the supreme branch of the government, for Randolph had announced that, should the impeachments fail, the President would remove the judges on the address of both houses of Congress. The removal of the present judges and the appointment of "unprincipled successors," he added, would complete the ruin of the nation.[86]

On the Louisiana Government Bill, the opposition of the Federalist extremists was limited to the clause which permitted the existence of slavery in the territory. In other respects the measure was satisfactory to them, for it set up a government in which the inhabitants were treated as residents of a conquered province and hence could not immediately exercise on national politics the

[83] Pickering MSS., Pickering to Rufus Putnam, Dec. 6; to John Taylor Gilman, Governor of New Hampshire, Dec. 20; to William Hull, Dec. 29; to Theophilus Parsons, Dec. 31, 1803; to Timothy Williams, Jan. 3; to Stephen Higginson, Jan. 6, 1804.

[84] Pickering MSS., Letters from William Barton, Thomas McKean, Andrew Ellicott, and others, Dec., 1803-Feb., 1804.

[85] *Ibid.*, Pickering to Higginson, Jan. 6, 1804.

[86] Henry Adams (ed.), *Documents relating to New England Federalism, 1800-15* (Boston, 1878), 343-46, Pickering to Lyman, Feb. 11, 1804.

influence which Pickering feared.   In the debates on the bill he took a stand definitely opposed to any extension of self-government to the territory.   He described its people as "incapable of performing the duties or enjoying the blessings of a free government."   "They are too ignorant to elect suitable men," he said.[87]   But the New England-ers found danger in the admission of slavery to the terri-tory.   They expressed no desire to free the slaves already in Louisiana, but wished to prevent the further growth of the institution.   Hillhouse thought slavery a serious evil and wished to check it wherever possible.   He held that it created a danger of revolt and that this danger was particularly serious in the New Orleans area where the blacks already outnumbered the whites.[88]   With this rea-soning Pickering agreed and he offered to support an amendment which would make the importation of slaves a criminal act.[89]   This amendment was lost.   Then Hill-house introduced a substitute which would restrict the privilege of importation to United States citizens who should enter the territory for actual settlement.   This was unacceptable to Pickering who was never willing to com-promise, but the Senate adopted the amendment by a heavy majority.[90]   The bill was then passed as amended.[91]

Obviously the real reasons for the opposition to the further admission of slavery were not those which Picker-ing and Hillhouse announced publicly.   The real force behind their efforts arose from their fear that Louisiana would eventually be a powerful ally of Virginia.   The territory was well adapted by climate to the use of slaves and permission to introduce them would lead to the popu-lation of the region by Southerners.   Furthermore, their political power would be enhanced by the slave representa-tion clause of the Constitution.   The Federalists under-stood this only too well and the repeal of that provision had already become part of their program.

The continued triumphs of the Republicans threw the Federalists into a condition of hopeless despair.   The measures which they had opposed so strenuously served

87 *Plumer's memorandum*, 111.
88 *Ibid.*, 113.
89 *Ibid.*, 121.
90 *Ibid.*, 132.
91 *Ibid.*, 146.

only to increase the popularity of Jefferson, a fact which
that astute leader did not fail to note. He boasted to
Monroe that the entire nation, with the exception of Delaware and the three New England states of Connecticut,
Massachusetts, and New Hampshire, had been won by
Republicanism and that even in New England the party
was gaining.[92] As the prospects for a revival of Federalism and a reassertion of New England's influence in the
Union grew blacker, the Federalist leaders turned to desperate measures. Late in January, 1804, when their
failure to halt the tide of Jeffersonianism was apparent,
the extreme Federalist delegation in Washington formulated plans for the secession of New England and undertook secretly to sound out the opinions of political leaders
in that section.

The suggestion of disunion was not new in New England. In 1796 when it appeared that Thomas Jefferson
might be elected to the Presidency, certain of the northern
leaders became alarmed and asserted, in private and in
public, that a severance of the Union would be preferable
to southern domination of the United States and to the
influence of France, exercised through the policies of Jefferson.[93] The election of John Adams put an end to further consideration of this project and it was not revived
in 1800 when Jefferson was actually elected. Yet some
men have seen in this incident the beginning of a long
and continuous plot to effect the separation of New England, a plot which existed secretly in the conversations of
a select group of leaders from 1796 until after the Hartford Convention in 1814, but which found overt expression only in the activities of the Federalists of New England in 1804, 1808, and 1814.[94] This opinion, however,

[92] Jefferson, *Works*, VIII, 286, Jefferson to Monroe, Jan. 8,
1804.

[93] Plumer, *Life of Plumer*, 282-83; J. C. Hamilton, *History of
the Republic* (7 vols., Philadelphia, 1864), VII, 772-73; Mathew
Carey, *The Olive Branch* (Philadelphia, 1814), preface to the
first edition. Timothy Dwight and Oliver Wolcott, Sr., were
the leaders who suggested disunion at this time, while the *Connecticut Courant* advocated it openly.

[94] This was the view of John Quincy Adams, William Plumer,
and Mathew Carey. See Adams, *New England Federalism*, 107-
339; *Life of Plumer*, 282-83; *Olive Branch*, preface to first edition.

does not rest upon substantial evidence and is based largely upon the views of men who were bitter enemies of the New England high Federalists. No one was more deeply involved in the plans of the Federalist leaders and in later years no one was more extreme in disunionist feeling than Timothy Pickering. Yet, until late in 1803, no trace or suggestion of secession can be found in his public or private writings. Not even the events of 1800 could arouse him to take that course.

While a definite plan to bring about New England secession did not emerge until January, 1804, the discussion over Louisiana in the fall of 1803 did bring forth numerous prophecies that the acquisition of this western territory would eventually disolve the Union. Some even went so far as to say that the Purchase had already destroyed the Union by upsetting the balance of states within the nation. William Plumer declared in October that it would compel the eastern states "to establish a separate and independent empire."[95] Christopher Gore was sure that it meant that the administration would rely entirely on western and southern support and "leave the Eastern States to perish . . . in poverty and disgrace."[96] It was this consideration that had led him to declare earlier that "Wise men should turn their thoughts to what is to be the next chapter in our every varying systems."[97] To Fisher Ames it seemed that "Our country is too big for union, ..."[98] In December, a few weeks after the fight over Louisiana, Pickering expressed a similar opinion when he wrote to Richard Peters:

"I will rather anticipate a new confederacy, exempt from the corrupt and corrupting influence and oppression of the aristocratic Democrats of the South. There will be—and our children at farthest will see it—a separation. The white and black population will mark the boundary. The British Provinces, even with the consent of Britain, will become members of the Northern Confederacy. A continued tyranny of the present ruling sect will precipitate that event. The patience of good citizens is now nearly exhausted."[99]

[95] Plumer, *Life of Plumer*, 285.
[96] King, *Life and correspondence of Rufus King*, IV, 334-35.
[97] *Ibid.*, 319-20.
[98] Ames, *Works*, I, 327-28.
[99] Adams, *New England Federalism*, 338; Lodge, *Cabot*, 441.

Even in the public prints, the idea of separation was voiced, for the *Salem Gazette* held that the "old Union" was already dissolved by the destruction of the old balance.[100] Nor was the opinion restricted to Federalists in New England, for William Rawle, a party leader in Pennsylvania, predicted that the northern states would "probably separate."[101]

From the expression of such sentiments as these, it was but a step to the discussion of an actual plan of secession. This step was taken by the little group of extremists in Washington. Besides Pickering, its prominent members were James Hillhouse, Uriah Tracy, William Plumer, and Roger Griswold. How many more may have been concerned in the matter is a subject for conjecture, but it seems unlikely that any others in Washington were taken very far into their confidence. At any rate, the active management of the affair was entirely in the hands of this circle who kept the business shrouded in secrecy. In private conversation they drew up their plans and then approached the party leaders outside of Congress. Without the approval of Hamilton, King, Cabot, and a host of lesser lights, the scheme had slight chance of success.

To George Cabot, the recognized leader of New England Federalism, Pickering first unfolded the project. In a long letter of January 29 he set forth the condition of the nation as it related to the fortunes of Federalism and its principles. Everywhere about him he saw men becoming "apostates, not to Federalism merely, but to virtue, religion, and good government." The attack on the judiciary, which had just begun, he believed a prelude to the destruction "of every influential Federalist and every man of considerable property, who is not of the reigning sect." For this condition he could find no remedy but separation.

"The people of the East," he said, "cannot reconcile their habits, views, and interests with those of the South and West. The latter are beginning to rule with a rod of iron. When not convenient to violate the Constitution, it must be altered; and it will be made to assume any shape as an instrument to crush the Federalists."

[100] Nov. 15, 1803.
[101] Pickering MSS., Rawle to Pickering, Jan. 5, 1804.

On the other hand, secession and the formation of a Northern Confederacy "would unite congenial characters." Having established the necessity and desirability of this course, he proceeded to outline the way in which it might be peacefully accomplished. Massachusetts, as the strongest Federalist state, must take the first step and he suggested that a declaration from the state legislature at its meeting in May would be appropriate. As the legislature of Connecticut was to meet at the same time and that of New Hampshire a little later, he felt sure that they would follow the lead of Massachusetts. But this was not enough. A purely New England Confederacy could not stand by itself and it would be necessary to secure the adherence of New York which would become the center of the Confederacy. If that could be accomplished, he predicted that New Jersey and Vermont would shortly join the new government. He predicted, too, that Canada and Nova Scotia would join the Confederacy "at no remote period, perhaps without delay, and with the assent of Great Britain." This would be followed by a treaty of amity and commerce between Great Britain and the Northern League which would be highly advantageous to both parties. He closed by asking Cabot whether he thought the scheme practicable and expedient.[102]

Cabot's reply indicated that little help was to be expected from that quarter. He appreciated the evils which the Senator had described, but he felt that separation would be no remedy, *"because the source of them is in the political theories of our country and in ourselves."* Democracy was gaining even in New England and he said, "I hold democracy in its natural operation, to be *the government of the worst."* He sympathized with the desire for separation and believed that it would inevitably come about at a later time, but his objection to it was that it would do no good unless democracy were also rooted out. To this reason for disapproving the plan he added another, that it was not practicable unless coming at a time when some extremely unpopular act of the administration, such as a war with England, would arouse a general revulsion against the government. Unless this

[102] Adams, *New England Federalism*, 338-42.

were the case, he held that any attempt at secession was bound to fail and that such failure could lead only to the control of New England by the Republicans.[103]

In this opinion Cabot was supported by other members of the Junto. Ames, Parsons, Higginson, and Lyman had been consulted and while all of them felt that the existing conditions were intolerable, all agreed that Cabot's view of the matter was correct.[104] Lyman, to whom Pickering had written directly to describe the same plan which he had outlined to Cabot,[105] admitted the existence of all the dangers emphasized by Pickering, but believed that an attempt at secession would result in disaster.[106] Higginson and Ames were equally dubious of its success and wrote that no effort should be made.[107]

While Pickering was sounding out the "Junto," his associates were corresponding with their friends in other parts of New England. Plumer wrote to Bradford Cilley, Oliver Peabody, and other New Hampshire leaders to ask their opinions of the project, and to urge them to make great efforts to maintain Federalist supremacy in the March election. Their replies were uniformly discouraging and Plumer learned that the people as a whole did not feel the necessity of action. He was told that commercial men deplored the possibility of secession as a measure that might ruin them. Such answers prompted him to write:

"The love of money will be our ruin. . . . If New England will not come out and separate from this mass of Southern corruption, she must partake of their plagues."[108]

At the same time, Griswold and Tracy were endeavoring to stir up the Connecticut Federalists.[109] From this state

103 Adams, *New England Federalism*, 346-49, Cabot to Pickering, Feb. 14, 1804.
104 *Ibid.*, 350, 353, 361-62, 365; Lyman to Pickering, Feb. 29; Cabot to Pickering, Mar. 7; Higginson to Pickering, Mar. 17; Ames to Pickering, Apr. 28, 1804.
105 *Ibid.*, 343-46, Pickering to Lyman, Feb. 11, 1804.
106 Adams, *New England Federalism*, 350, Lyman to Pickering, Feb. 29, 1804.
107 *Ibid.*, 361-62, 365, Higginson to Pickering, Mar. 17, 1804; Ames to Pickering, Apr. 28, 1804.
108 Plumer, *Life of Plumer*, 285-88.
109 Adams, *New England Federalism*, 338-42, Pickering to Cabot, Jan. 29, 1804.

came a more favorable response, and Judge Tapping Reeve reported that there was "a very general opinion" that some means must be devised to escape the ruin which threatened party and section. In his mind the major difficulty seemed to lie in deciding on a method by which secession might be accomplished. On this point he confessed that he was wholly in the dark, but he suggested that the issue might be raised over the pending constitutional amendment, on the ground that its passage by two-thirds of those present in each house rather than two-thirds of the entire membership was unconstitutional. As a preliminary step he favored a "bold address" from the Federalist Congressmen to their constituents. If this were issued before the state elections of that spring, he believed that it would be of great effect in preparing the people for further measures. It should be followed, he said, by appropriate declarations from the legislatures. Then, if the responses of the people were favorable, the final step might be taken.[110]

In spite of the apparent lack of support, the little band of conspirators was not willing to give up its plan. Only Connecticut showed any strong desire to go through with the project of secession. The Massachusetts and New Hampshire party leaders had expressed their disapproval and it was soon learned that no help could be expected from Hamilton and King in New York. Their opposition was unreservedly brought out by the next stage in the conspiracy which proposed a union with a faction of northern Republicans under the leadership of Aaron Burr. Burr was then a candidate for the governorship of New York and it was hoped that his election, with the support of Federalist voters, would lead to a fusion of the Federalists and certain elements of the Republican party in the northern states that would produce a majority party strong enough to effect secession. Such was the tenor of the proposals made by Pickering and Griswold in March. To Lyman, Pickering declared, "This will break the Democratic phalanx of that state, and prepare the way for the contemplated event." To King, he expressed his

---

[110] Adams, *New England Federalism*, 342-43, T[apping] R[eeve] to U[riah] T[racy], Feb. 7, 1804.

opinion that it would enable New York and New Jersey
to unite with the five New England states if separation
should take place; without separation he saw no hope for
the northern states to escape the influence of the Virginia
Republicans. Apparently oblivious to the advice he had
received from Massachusetts, he asserted, "I do not know
one reflecting Nov.Anglian who is not anxious for the
Great Event." Its success, he believed, was sure, unless
"improper delay" should defeat it. Griswold was some-
what more hesitant, for he distrusted Burr and feared
that many Federalists would not have confidence in him.
Furthermore, all of Burr's remarks had been so guarded
that Griswold could feel no real assurance that the Vice-
President, if successful in New York, would follow the
course desired by the New England leaders. Nevertheless, he favored the support of Burr.

"If we remain inactive," he said, "our ruin is certain.
By supporting Burr, we gain some support, though of doubt-
ful nature, and of which we have cause enough to be jealous.
In short I see nothing else for us."[111]

Nothing could illustrate better the desperation of the
Federalists in Congress than this plan. While leaders
outside had disapproved of secession from the first, they
now became actively opposed to it. Even before the proposals of Pickering and Griswold were made known, the
acute Hamilton came to the conclusion that Burr's can-
didacy was predicated on Federalist support and that it
might lead to the erection of a Northern Confederacy
with Aaron Burr as president. The elevation of his arch-
enemy to a post of such importance was for him an
unbearable thought, and on February tenth he appeared
at a Federalist meeting in Albany to oppose plans for
the support of Burr. Pointing out that jealousy of Jefferson and Virginia was the only reason for giving Federalist aid to Burr, he declared that these extreme views
were

"leading to an opinion, that a dismemberment of the

111 Adams, *New England Federalism*, 354-60: Griswold to
Wolcott, Mar. 11, 1804; Pickering to Lyman, Mar. 14, 1804.
King, *Life and correspondence of Rufus King*, IV, 364-66, Pick-
ering to King, Mar. 4, 1804.

Union was expedient" and that "it would probably suit Mr. Burr's views to promote this result, to be the head of the Northern Confederacy; and placed at the head of the state of New York, no man would be more likely to succeed."[112]

That Hamilton's view was correct was soon borne out by the New York *Morning Chronicle* which asserted that the only way to restore northern influence in the Union was to elect Aaron Burr governor of New York.[113] Following his declaration at Albany, Hamilton approached Rufus King with a proposal that he run for the governorship in order to divert the Federalist vote from Burr.[114] King, however, felt that the objections to this course were "insurmountable" and he refused to run.[115]

However, Hamilton continued to do all in his power to defeat Burr. What his real motives were is difficult to say. His admirers are at one in declaring that his reason was love of the Union, but it is significant that he exerted no influence to halt the plans of the secessionists until Burr's name became involved in their schemes. His hatred of Burr is well known to have been so strong that nothing could have been more distasteful to him than the success of his ancient enemy. On the other hand, it seems scarcely fair, in the face of his known political principles, to attribute his opposition solely to his enmity for Burr. Yet his support of the Union was not based simply upon patriotism, for in 1804 patriotism did not imply the same belief in a united American nation that it has in more recent times. Instead, it is far more likely that he agreed with Cabot in not condemning disunion *per se,* but in opposing it because it would prove no cure for democracy. He was convinced that disunion under Burr's leadership would only promote the triumph of "Jacobinism" in the North.[116] Another factor worthy of consideration is that the success of a plan originating with

[112] Hamilton, *History of the Republic*, VII, 770-72, quoting MSS. notes among Hamilton's papers on "Reasons why it is desirable that Mr. Lansing rather than Col. Burr should succeed."

[113] *Ibid.*, 777, quoting N. Y. *Morning Chronicle*, Feb. 22, 1804.

[114] King, *Life and correspondence of Rufus King*, IV, 351-53, Hamilton to King, Feb. 24, 1804.

[115] *Ibid.*, 353, King to Hamilton, Feb. 24, 1804.

[116] Hamilton, *History of the Republic*, VII, 770-72.

the Pickering group would have destroyed his leadership of the party, a result scarcely to his liking. There is no single explanation of his course, but rather, his action must be attributed to a variety of motives, some arising out of principle, others out of the considerations of party politics.

Cabot also threw his weight against the election of Burr and in March wrote to Rufus King to condemn the union of the Federalists with the Vice-President. While he could still sympathize with Pickering and Griswold in resenting the triumphs of Jeffersonianism, he was convinced that separation was no proper remedy. *"Our evils must be borne until their intolerability generates their cure,"* he wrote. As for the New York election, he declared, "I should rejoice to see Burr win the race in your state, but I cannot approve of aid being given him by any of the *leading* Federalists."[117]

Meanwhile the conspirators went on with their plans. At Washington Burr extended to them as much encouragement as he could without definitely committing himself to their program. On occasion he entertained them at dinner and drew from them statements of their belief in disunion. Although he left them with the impression that he approved their plan, he carefully avoided any specific agreement. William Plumer, who was present at these dinners, went away convinced that Burr would support the project, but on analyzing his remarks, he realized that the Vice-President had said nothing "that necessarily implied his approbation."[118]

With so much discussion of the possibility of northern secession, it was inevitable that news of the plot should come to the notice of those who were not intended to hear of it. Among others, John Quincy Adams learned of it and a few weeks later had the news confirmed in the course of some conversations with Rufus King in New York.[119] Gideon Granger also learned of what was trans-

[117] Lodge, *Cabot*, 345-46, Cabot to King, Mar. 17, 1804. Also printed in Adams, *New England Federalism*, 362-64, and King, *Life and correspondence of Rufus King*, IV, 370-71.

[118] *Plumer's memorandum*, 517-18. ". . . Perhaps no man's language was ever so apparently explicit, and at the same time so covert and indefinite," was Plumer's opinion of Burr.

[119] Adams, *New England Federalism*, 147.

piring and reported his discovery to Jefferson, but the
President refused to be alarmed at the prospect of this
"bastard system of federorepublicanism."   He was convinced that the mass of the Republicans would remain
true to the principles of the party and thwart the ambi-
tions of its enemies.[120]

After the close of the Congressional session, the Federalist plotters gathered in New York to continue their
conversations and complete their preparations.   Before
they could proceed with their plans, two tasks remained
to be performed: to secure a definite agreement with Burr
and to win over Hamilton and King.   In each case they
were unsuccessful.   Burr was as evasive as ever.   Griswold called on him on April fourth, but received no further committment than a promise that he would "adminis-
ter the government [of New York] in a manner satisfactory to the Federalists" and an opinion that either "the
Northern States must be governed by Virginia, or govern
Virginia."[121]   Yet Griswold and his friends continued
their efforts in Burr's behalf with the result that the
greater part of the New York Federalists voted for him
in utter disregard of Hamilton's pleas.   But Burr was
weak within his own party and consequently lost the governorship.   Although he blamed Hamilton for it, his defeat was due primarily to the strength of the Clinton
Republicans.[122]

At the home of Rufus King, the confederates held several conversations in the course of which they unfolded
their plans and their belief in the necessity of secession.[123]
Pickering attempted personally to convert Hamilton and
King to his way of thinking, but neither one would give
his approval to the plan.[124]   They deplored the existence
of conditions which diminished the influence of the

[120] Jefferson, *Works*, VIII, 298, Jefferson to the Postmaster-
General, Apr. 16, 1804.
[121] King, *Life and correspondence of Rufus King*, IV, 356,
King's record of conversations with Oliver Wolcott, spring,
1804.
[122] Adams, *History of the United States*, II, 184-85.
[123] King, *Life and correspondence of Rufus King*, 355-56,
King's record of conversations with Oliver Wolcott, spring,
1804.
[124] Adams, *New England Federalism*, 147-48.

northern states in the Union, but they felt that secession would be "a remedy more desperate than any possible disease."[125] Failure to secure either a definite agreement with Burr or the support of Hamilton and King led the Pickering group to hold its plans temporarily in abeyance. Arrangements were made to hold a meeting in Boston in the early autumn when further measures could be discussed.[126]

But the meeting in Boston was never held. The duel between Hamilton and Burr in July made the latter an outcast and forever unacceptable to the Federalists, while Hamilton became a hero and a martyr whose words were gospel throughout New England and New York. His opinion opposed to disunion now carried more weight in extreme Federalist circles than his influence did while he was still alive. If he had lived and had gone to the Boston meeting, as the plotters said he had promised to do, he would have thrown all his influence against disunion, but he could not have so completely stifled all further discussion as this event did. On the night before the duel he penned a short note to Theodore Sedgwick, expressing his final opinion that,

"Dismemberment of our Empire will be a clear sacrifice of great positive advantages without any counterbalancing good; administering no relief to our real disease, which is Democracy: the poison of which by a subdivision, will only be more concentrated in each part, and consequently the more virulent."[127]

These words had the effect which Hamilton undoubtedly intended and no more was heard of the plot to create a Northern Confederacy with Aaron Burr as president.

Before Hamilton's death, his friend, King, had set out for Boston to visit several friends there and, incidentally, to dissuade the New Englanders from any further attempts at secession. In Boston, and later in Salem and Newburyport, the Federalists gave him a royal welcome. What passed between the leaders at that time is not a

[125] Adams, *New England Federalism*, 147-148.
[126] Plumer, *Life of Plumer*, 290-92.
[127] Adams, *New England Federalism*, 365; Hamilton, *History of the Republic*, VII, 824; King, *Life and correspondence of Rufus King*, IV, 360; Plumer, *Life of Plumer*, 307.

matter of record, but it is a fair surmise that it had much
to do with the abandonment of the more extreme plans
of the Federalists. By this time, Hamilton's death was
known and there can be little doubt that King made effective use of what he knew to be the dead leader's wishes.[128]

Thus ended the plan for the formation of a Northern
Confederacy, a plan which Pickering held to be the only
real remedy for the declining influence of New England
and the only escape from the policies and principles of
Thomas Jefferson, which he sincerely believed to be
ruinous. It began and ended as a plot known only to a
small and select circle. Years passed before its details
ever saw the light of day. When that occurred, all those
who had been most closely connected with it were dead.
Pickering himself never mentioned the incident again,
save possibly to his closest friends in private conversation. While the plan remained a secret, it is interesting
to note that many of its details, considered then as steps
toward the formation of a Northern Confederacy, were
converted into measures of opposition to the Embargo in
1808. The bold appeal of Federalist Congressmen to
their constituents, the action of the state legislatures, and
the reliance on the likelihood of English support were all
prominent features of the later movement. While there
was probably no direct connection between the two epi-
sodes in the sense of the existence of a continuous plot to
secure the secession of New England, the methods and
ideas developed in 1804 provided a line of action in 1808.

The plot of 1804 had no chance of success. It could
not even have served as an effective threat to Republican
supremacy. In spite of the acute discontent of Pickering
and his commercial friends, the policies of Jefferson were
constantly gaining in popularity, even in New England.
On returning to Salem in the summer of 1804, Jacob
Crowninshield wrote to Jefferson,

"Permit me to embrace this occasion of assuring you that

[128] King, *Life and correspondence of Rufus King*, IV, 417-20.
On this occasion, the group that had bought Pickering's Pennsylvania lands turned them over to Hamilton's heirs as a way
of expressing their appreciation of his services and of accept-
ing some responsibility for his family which had been left in
straitened circumstances.

the republican principles are gaining ground in the Eastern States. The friends of your excellent Administration increase daily. The general measures which have been pursued are considered wise and proper, and if calumny has spread her vile insinuations we may be certain that Federalism gains no converts, but on the contrary experience demonstrates her cause to be in a rapid decline."[129]

Although this was the testimony of one of Pickering's political opponents, it must be accepted as substantially correct, for in the fall of 1804, Massachusetts gave a majority of 3000 for the "Virginia ticket" in the national election.[130] The cause of Federalism had suffered an eclipse in New England and it was not to be revived as an effective political force until the reaction against the Embargo in 1808-09 gave it the character of a popular movement. For Pickering, the failure of Federalism meant that he was reduced to the place of an ineffective minority leader. He had been brought back to politics to lead a Federalist revival and as a means to that end he had adopted a desperate and extreme course which was doomed to failure. That failure served only to make him more bitter than ever against Jefferson[131] and his party and to leave him awaiting a more favorable opportunity.

[129] Jefferson MSS., Library of Congress, Crowninshield to Jefferson, July 14, 1804.

[130] *Salem Gazette*, Nov. 16, 1804.

[131] His bitterness is well displayed in the following quotation from the Pickering MSS., Pickering to Robert Liston, Mar. 19, 1805: "Until Mr. Jefferson's real character was displayed, I had never felt the force of the repeated denunciation, 'Wo unto you, scribes & pharisees, hypocrites!' for in hypocrisy are combined all things false, base, and detestable in the human character. . . . The future Historian will hang him in gibbets— and there I leave him."

PICKERING AND THE EMBARGO.

By Hervey Putnam Prentiss.

From the failure of the Federalist plot of 1804 until the latter part of 1807, the public career of Timothy Pickering was marked by great inactivity. Although his feeling against the Republican administration became increasingly bitter,[1] his opposition was futile, for there was no popular issue of any consequence which could give him the opportunity to direct a Federalist reaction against Jefferson. In spite of the difficulties of his second administration, the President's conduct of public affairs remained popular. In Massachusetts its popularity was steadily gaining and in 1807 the Republicans won complete control of the state, as James Sullivan was elected governor and his party secured majorities in both houses of the legislature.[2] In 1805 Pickering had been re-elected to the Senate, but the narrow majority given him by the Massachusetts House of Representatives was proof of the declining strength of Federalism in the state.[3] Under such circumstances in his own state, and with the Federalists failing to gain elsewhere, he could be merely the leader of an ineffective opposition which was forced to wait for a more favorable occasion to open a concerted attack on the administration.

[1] The intensity of his feeling is revealed in his letters, of which the following excerpt is typical. "His [Jefferson's] administration has always had *deception* for its principle. But the exposure of his baseness has commenced—it will be continued—and he must sink under it. So perish all political hypocrites!" (Pickering MSS., Pickering to Fisher Ames, Apr. 1, 1806.)

[2] *Salem Gazette*, Apr. 28, May 29, 1807.

[3] *Ibid.*, Feb. 8, 1805.

(37)

That occasion came in December, 1807, in the passage
of the Embargo, which Pickering regarded as the crowning act of Jefferson's pro-French and anti-commercial
policy. He had long been convinced that the administration was acting under the dictation of France[4] and that
its measures, taken ostensibly in defence of American
rights, were in reality designed to hinder the English,
whom he believed to be fighting the battles of civilization
and liberty against their enemies, the French under
Napoleon.[5] That in the course of these battles Great
Britain should find it necessary to seize neutral ships and
impress neutral seamen seemed to him inconsequential.
If this involved actual injuries to the rights of neutral
nations, he was sure that Britain would in due time make
proper compensation for them.

"Why, then should We be so ardent in our *reclamations*
(pardon the Gallicism—no other word is at hand) against
the English on the score of neutral commerce?" he asked,
"Why add to her distress, when she is fighting our battles
with her own blood and treasure with some aid in the latter,
from us? How much more would it cost to maintain a direct
war for ourselves? — But England has ungenerously as un-
wisely ensnared our merchants, & with mercantile jealousy,
& privateering rapacity, seized their property: granted. So
they did in 1793: and made reparation for the wrong. So
they will again, if our Government, coerced by the prevailing
sentiment of the people, should institute a *proper mission*
to the Court of London."[6]

This attitude was brought out unmistakably during the
discussion of the *Chesapeake affair*. Not even this direct
affront to American honor could convince Pickering that
the United States should take any steps in its own defence

[4] King, *Life and Correspondence of Rufus King*, IV, 476, Pickering to King, Jan. 13, 1806, "I apprehend that there is sufficient
pliability in the administration to yield whatever the 'master'
of our sister Republic shall demand."

[5] Pickering MSS., Pickering to Robert Liston, Mar. 19, 1805,
"Of the nations upon earth, it is most important for ours and
yours to be on good terms; they are the only nations who
know and enjoy political and civil liberty; our wants are recip-
rocal and we are peculiarly of one blood and one flesh."

[6] *Ibid.*, Pickering to Fisher Ames, Feb. 2, 1806.

which might inconvenience the British. On the contrary, he took the position that Captain Barron of the *Chesapeake* had been wrong in refusing to surrender the men whom he knew, as Pickering believed, to be British deserters.[7] Although the Senator admitted that the Captain of the *Leopard* had violated American neutrality in forcing the *Chesapeake* to submit to search, he declared that the British had offered sufficient apology in disavowing the attack and promising to abstain from searching ships of war in the future. The President, however, had coupled a demand for the complete abandonment of impressment with his insistence upon an apology for this insult to the sovereignty of the United States. As Pickering believed that Great Britain had a right to the services of her own seamen wherever they might be found, he asserted that the administration's attitude was indefensible, that it was "a mere *stalking-horse,* behind which they direct their impolite and malicious attacks on Britain" in order to "increase Mr. Jefferson's ill-acquired and unmerited popularity."[8]

Before this affair had been satisfactorily settled, Jefferson hastily recommended an embargo to Congress, and both houses passed the bill by overwhelming majorities.[9] Pickering immediately concluded that the measure had been designed by the President under Napoleon's dictation as a means of extending the principles of the Continental System to America. It was his belief that Bonaparte had informed Jefferson, through the American minister at Paris, that he would no longer tolerate neutrality, and that the administration had chosen the Embargo as a means of conforming to the Emperor's wishes.[10] Although the law was operative against all nations trading with the United States, the Massachusetts Senator, conscious of the fact that the greater part of American commerce was with Great Britain and her colonies, believed that it was aimed primarily at that nation. Admitting that it would

[7] Pickering MSS., Pickering to S. P. Gardner, Nov. 18, 1807.
[8] *Ibid.*, Pickering to S. P. Gardner, Dec. 10, 1807.
[9] *Annals of Congress*, 10th Congress, 1st session, 50-51.
[10] Pickering MSS., Pickering to Timothy Williams, Dec. 21, 1807.

affect the French and Spanish colonies, he declared that
that would not cause Napoleon to shed "a single tear" if
only Great Britain would be "materially reduced" by it.
Hence, he concluded:

"I have considered the embargo as only a new mode (in
conformity with the Emperor's wishes or demands) of shut-
ting the ports of the U. States against the manufactures and
products of the British dominions immediately, or, by aggra-
vating mutual hostile feelings, in good time, to produce a
war."[11]

Later, when it became necessary to defend his assertion
that French influence had produced the Embargo, Pickering sought his proof in the circumstances under which the
law had been passed. The President had summoned both
Houses in secret session to consider his recommendation
of an embargo. With his message he had submitted four
documents, two of which were not to be published and
were to be returned to him. In one of them, a letter
from Champagny, the French minister of foreign affairs,
to Armstrong, the American minister at Paris, occurred
the statement that the Berlin Decree had been in force
for several months without accomplishing the expected
results, and that the Emperor had declared that "its
execution must be more compete to render it more effec-
tual." This, Pickering construed as a thinly-veiled order
that the United States should co-operate with France in
striking a blow at British commerce. If this were not the
case, he could see no reason for the secrecy which the President had demanded.[12] This argument, however, was only
a rationalization produced to support his charge of French
influence, for it did not appear until February, 1808, when
he decided to make a public appeal for support in an at-

[11] *Ibid.*, Pickering to Timothy Williams, Dec. 31, 1807.
[12] Pickering, *Letter . . . exhibiting to his constituents a view
of the imminent danger of an unnecessary and ruinous war*
(Boston, 1808). Pickering offered this opinion on several later
occasions, notably in a speech supporting the repeal of the
Embargo in the fall of 1808 (*Annals of Congress*, 10th, 2nd,
175-94), in his *Address to the People of the United States* in
1811, and in his *Review of the Correspondence between John
Adams and William Cunningham* in 1824.

tack on the administration. Although he had been engaged
for weeks in denouncing the Embargo to his friends, this
account did not appear in any of his private letters. That
he was sincere in believing that Jefferson had accepted the
dictation of Napoleon cannot be doubted, but that belief
was the result, not of the events immediately connected
with the passage of the Embargo, but of his own deep-
seated prejudices against the President and of his own
intense partiality for England.

As a matter of fact, however, Jefferson had proposed
the Embargo because at that moment Great Britain was
increasing the severity of her measures to restrict neutral
trade. An Order in Council of November 11, 1807, had
declared a blockade of the European coast from Copen-
hagen to Trieste. It is certain that Jefferson knew this
and was influenced by it, but as he had not been officially
informed, he could not make use of it in his recommendation to Congress.[13] In all probability Pickering knew
of it, too, for on December 18, the day of the President's
message, the *National Intelligencer* had announced that
official news of the order was expected.[14] Furthermore,
Timothy Williams had written to him on December 12
to say that he had just received from his brother, Samuel,
in London, under the date of November 9, a letter in
which it was stated that the British were about to issue
such an order.[15] Only Pickering's hostility to Jefferson
and his love for England could have prevented him from
seeing that the British Order was the immediate occasion
for the President's message.

Yet, in spite of all his condemnations of the Embargo,
Pickering saw in it a golden opportunity for Federalism.
On the day that the House of Representatives passed the
act, he wrote to his nephew, Timothy Williams:

"Our affairs are hastening to a crisis. Wickedness and

[13] Henry Adams, *History of the United States*, IV, 168-70.
[14] J. Q. Adams, *A letter to the Hon. Harrison Gray Otis, a
member of the senate of Massachusetts, on the present state of
our national affairs, with remarks upon Mr. Pickering's letter
to the governor of the Commonwealth* (Boston, 1808), 9.
[15] Pickering MSS., Timothy Williams to Pickering, Dec. 12,
1807.

folly are united to bring misery, if not ruin, upon our country. I look forward, however, to at least a great *possible* good to flow from much evil."[16]

He knew, of course, that the Embargo would react disastrously upon the merchants of New England and that, if continued long enough, it would produce distress among other classes of the population as well. Out of this discontent created by Republican measures, he and his friends might direct a Federalist revival that would restore the northern states to their former position of power and, incidentally, place him and his friends in high office. Hence, he conceived it to be his mission to arouse the latent forces of Federalism and to undertake any project that promised defeat to the Embargo and disaster to Jefferson.

His judgment of the effect which the Embargo would have upon New England, especially upon its merchants, was substantially correct. Within a fortnight, George Cabot informed him that the "evils of the Embargo" had already been felt and that "threats of violence" were circulating among the people. It was his opinion, too, that the Embargo would "bring greater immediate distress than war."[17] To Pickering, that must have been indeed encouraging, for it was out of such distress that he hoped to build his Federalist revival. From New York, Rufus King wrote words of similar import, declaring, ". . . the Embargo has already produced distressing consequences, and these must increase daily."[18] From Timothy Williams came further encouragement which strengthened the Senator's belief that a Federalist reaction was possible.

"Mr. Jefferson," he wrote, "has imposed an Embargo,— to please France and Beggar us! Let it remain 3 or 4 months as I hope it will; and I am mistaken if it produce not good to the federal party and friends of peace if they conduct with prudence and bring down on Mr. Jefferson 'curses loud and deep.' "[19]

[16] *Ibid.*, Pickering to Timothy Williams, Dec. 22, 1807.
[17] H. C. Lodge, *Life and Letters of George Cabot* (Boston, 1877), 374-75, Cabot to Pickering, Dec. 31, 1807.
[18] Pickering MSS., King to Pickering, Dec. 31, 1807.
[19] *Ibid.*, Williams to Pickering, Jan. 1, 1808.

Writing in a similar vein, Benjamin Goodhue reported
that Federalists looked upon the Embargo as a "most
ridiculous and wicked measure" and declared that he was
"one among many who expect much good from it by bringing execration on the heads of its authors."[20]

Sentiments of this nature were not confined to the
private correspondence of Federalist politicians and merchants, for the party press of the New England seaports
took up the hue and cry against the administration. The
Salem Gazette proclaimed that the purpose of the Embargo was "to throw the whole mercantile class into the
water, to make sport for the great in beholding who in
the struggle for life will sink and who swim."[21] More
hopeful was "Curtius," a writer in the *Columbian Centinel,* who, though he denounced the Embargo, gave his
opinion that it was "the instrument chosen by heaven to
instruct while it chastizes," and predicted that it would be
the means of restoring Federalism.[22] So common was this
strong talk that the Republican governor of Massachusetts,
James Sullivan, warned the people of the state in his
address to the legislature at its January session that opposition to a law must never be carried to the point of
sedition.[23] Alarmed by the Federalist agitation, he feared
that there was a plot on foot to sever New England from
the Union, and he reported to the President that there
was much talk of a "division between the southern and
northern states." As a remedy, he suggested that Jefferson
should fill the federal courts in New England with judges
loyal to the administration.[24]

Small wonder, then, that Pickering was encouraged to
continue his plans for a concerted opposition to the administration and its Embargo. By January 19 he was writing
to King:

"You know the hostility of Jefferson and Virginians and
other Southern men to our carrying trade. . . . If Mr. J.

[20] Pickering MSS., Goodhue to Pickering, Jan. 19, 1808.
[21] Jan. 5, 1808.
[22] Jan. 23, 1808.
[23] *Salem Register*, Jan. 9, 1808.
[24] Jefferson MSS., Sullivan to Jefferson, Jan. 7, 1808, quoted in
L. M. Sears, *Jefferson and the Embargo* (Durham, N. C., 1927),
58.

can prevent the clamours of the farmers and soothe the manufacturers by giving them monopolies, will he be persuaded to continue the embargo to the destruction of the navigation of the Northern States? and will the latter sit still with folded arms and submit to ruin? A union of sentiment in the six eastern states would controul the folly and insidious Views of the East and prescribe a salutary policy for the Union."[25]

The suggestion did not elicit the enthusiastic support of King, who passed it by without comment. Nevertheless, Pickering remained convinced that it was his duty to call upon the northern Federalists to unite to defeat Jefferson and the Embargo. With that intention in mind, he prepared a public letter to Governor Sullivan to urge that the Massachusetts legislature take the first step toward the formation of a northern union. As if in justification of his course, he wrote again to King, saying:

"We must have a union of Northern Interests, to control the predelictions and counteract the fears of Jefferson, & overthrow Virginian domination."[26]

The letter to Sullivan was an inflammatory document designed as a call to the northern Federalists to secure the defeat of the Embargo through direct action of the state governments. In it, Pickering set forth his view of the policy of the administration. Paying no attention whatever to the Order in Council of November 11 as a cause of the Embargo, he said that the administration had given three reasons for urging the passage of the law: the impressment of American seamen; England's prohibition of neutral shipping to enemy ports; and the attack on the *Chesapeake.* Declaring that these reasons were merely "pretenses," he asserted that only the perversity of the administration had prevented the satisfactory settlement of these questions. On impressment, he insisted that Great Britain was willing to adopt any arrangement that could be devised to secure *"the seamen who are her own subjects"* and at the same time exempt American sailors from seizure. He justified the attempt to stop neutral trade

25 King, *Life and Correspondence of Rufus King,* V, 63-64.
26 *Ibid.,* 78-81, Pickering to King, Feb. 26, 1808.

with France on the ground that neutral ships became practically the allies of France when her own traders were driven from the ocean. As to the *Chesapeake* incident, he maintained that the British would have healed the breach *"if our own government would suffer it to be healed."* Contemptuously brushing aside these pretences, he offered his own theory as he asked:

"Has the French Emperor declared that he will have no neutrals? Has he required that *our ports,* like those of his vassal states in Europe, *be shut against British commerce?* Is the Embargo a *substitute,* a *milder form* of compliance, with that harsh demand, which if exhibited in its naked and insulting aspect, the American people might yet resent? Are we still to be kept profoundly ignorant of the declarations and avowed designs of the French Emperor, although these may strike at our liberty and independence? And in the meantime are we, by a thousand irritations, by cherishing prejudices, and bv exciting fresh resentments, to be drawn gradually into a war with Great Britain? Why amid the extreme anxiety of the public mind is it still kept upon the rack of fearful expectation by the President's portentous silence respecting the French despatches? In this conceal-ment there is danger. In this concealment must be wrapt the real cause of the embargo. On any other supposition it is inexplicable."[27]

Having thus implied that the administration was be-traying the interests of the nation, he pointed to the remedy.

"I declare to you," he wrote, "that I have no confidence in the wisdom or correctness of our publick measures: that our country is in imminent danger; that it is essential to the public safety, that the blind confidence in our Rulers should cease; that the State Legislature should know the facts and reasons on which important general laws are founded: *and especially that those States whose farms are on the ocean, and whose harvests are gathered in every sea,*

[27] Pickering, *Letter from the Hon. Timothy Pickering, a senator of the United States from the state of Massachusetts, exhibiting to his constituents a view of the imminent danger of an unnecessary and ruinous war; addressed to His Excellency James Sullivan, Governor of the said state* (Boston, 1808), 11.

should immediately and seriously consider how to preserve them. — Nothing but the sense of the commercial states, clearly and emphatically expressed, will save them from ruin."[28]

Here, then, was an appeal from the national Congress to the legislatures of the commercial states to take such action as would nullify the Embargo or force the administration to repeal it. Although addressed to Governor Sullivan and the Massachusetts legislature, the letter was obviously intended for publication. There was no chance that the Republican government of the state would take any action in response to the Senator's suggestion, for it had already adopted resolutions approving the course of the national administration.[29] However, the state election was approaching, and it was planned to publish this appeal, if refused by Sullivan and the legislature, as a means of arousing the voters to return the Federalists to power and thus begin the anti-Embargo reaction for which Pickering hoped. How far he wished this reaction to go is impossible to say. His enemies, some of whom knew of his activities in 1804, believed that his real purpose was to secure the secession of New England and the formation of a northern confederacy under British protection.[30] If such were his purpose, it was guarded well, for the language of his letter did not imply secession, although it clearly suggested nullification. Nor did he, in his private correspondence, intimate that he was aiming at the eventual secession of the northern states. As he was not given to hiding his thoughts, it seems likely, then, that his only purpose at the moment was to produce a party revolution in Massachusetts that would enable that state to take the lead in a Federalist revival. Having once accomplished the local party revolution, he might take any one of three courses to restore the influence of his party faction: the revival of the national Federalist party as a real political force, the defeat of the administration by

[28] *Ibid.*, 11-13.
[29] *Salem Gazette*, Feb. 13, 1808.
[30] Adams, *New England Federalism*, 195-96; Jefferson MSS., James Sullivan to Jefferson, Apr. 2, 1808, quoted in Sears, *Jefferson and the Embargo*, 68.

the Federalist minority through the medium of the nullification of the Embargo in the commercial states, or the
secession of New England. Which of these courses he
would choose would depend in large part on the state of
public opinion as revealed by the controversy that was
sure to follow.

   Sullivan naturally refused to submit the Senator's letter
to the legislature and returned it to him rather abruptly.[31]
As this was what Pickering had expected, he was already
prepared to appeal directly to the people of Massachusetts
over the head of the governor. Immediately after post-
ing his letter of February 16 to Sullivan, he had sent
another copy of the document to George Cabot with the
request that he publish it if it met his approval and if
it were not given to the legislature within a reasonable
length of time.[32] Cabot fell in with the plan immediately. Believing that "This excellent address is well calculated to arouse us from our apathy," he waited until
March 9 and then had it published as a pamphlet of
which 5,000 copies were distributed among the voters of
the state.[33] Not knowing that Cabot had already approved his original suggestion, Pickering, upon receiving
Sullivan's answer, wrote again to his fellow-Federalist for
advice. Admitting that there might be some doubts as
to the expediency of publication, he concluded in charac-
teristic fashion:

   ". . . may not the consideration that the governor and
his friends may misrepresent the affair, not only prejudicially
to me, but to the Federal cause, which is the cause of our
country, *demand* its publication."[34]

When he learned that Cabot had already taken action,
his satisfaction knew no limits and he suggested that more
editions of his letter be struck off and that Sullivan's refusal and his own reply to it be added to the pamphlet.[35]
   The effect of publication upon the Federalists was just

31 Lodge, *Cabot*, 380, Pickering to Cabot, Mar. 10, 1808.
32 *Ibid.*, 379, Cabot to Pickering, Mar. 3, 1808.
33 *Ibid.*, 380, Cabot to Pickering, Mar. 9, 1808.
34 *Ibid.*, 380-82, Pickering to Cabot, Mar. 11, 1808.
35 *Ibid.*, 387-89, Pickering to Cabot, Mar. 16, 1808.

what Pickering and Cabot had hoped. The pamphlet was reprinted again and again, as local politicians sought additional copies to distribute among their followers and as the editors of the party papers published it in their columns.[36]   From Federalist editors, the letter drew the highest praise, as they urged their readers to study it with care.   Typical of their extravagant comment was the plea of the *Newburyport Herald:*

"Whether Republicans or Federalists — read this letter — throw aside all party feelings and party animosity—read it as independent Americans—as men anxious to preserve the invaluable constitution which the great *Washington* has left you, and as men watchful to hold and cherish the rights and liberties to which you are entitled as the most important section of the Union."[37]

At the same time, Federalist gatherings in various parts of the state adopted laudatory resolutions which stamped Pickering's plea with the unmistakable marks of party approval and urged that the Federalists rise to protest against the Embargo and that, as a practical means to the defeat of that unpopular measure, they elect Christopher Gore as governor in place of the Republican Sullivan.[38]

The Republicans responded immediately with a counter-attack.   Sullivan had given due publicity to his refusal to entertain Pickering's proposal and this had been hailed by his party as a sign of firmness and vigor.[39]   A few days later, when he saw the tremendous popularity which Pickering's pamphlet was winning, he undertook to state his side of the case more fully in a public letter which condemned the Senator's proposal as "a seditious, disorganizing production" and justified his own refusal to communicate it to the General Court on the ground that it "would transfer all the debates of the national legislature from Washington to Boston."

[36] Bentley, *Diary*, III, 351.   Bentley estimated that 100,000 copies appeared before the April election.
[37] *Newburyport Herald*, Mar. 15, 1808.
[38] *Salem Gazette*, Mar. 25, Apr. 1, 1808, quoting resolutions of Federalists of Northampton, Newburyport, and Salem.
[39] *Salem Register*, Mar. 16, 1808.

"Each state having the same claim," he said, "the national government must cease to exist. . . . If there ever was an attempt in its nature and consequence tending to sedition and rebellion, this is one."[40]

The argument of this letter shortly became the basis of the Republican appeal to re-elect Governor Sullivan as the most practical way of demonstrating that Massachusetts was still behind the Jefferson administration and not ready to follow Pickering's lead in projects of nullification. Republican assemblies, responsive to the Governor's plea, adopted resolutions declaring Pickering's appeal "degrading to the country, and of an incendiary nature,"[41] and condemning it as a "scandalous and disorganizing libel on the government of the United States" which would degrade "the character of a Senator to that of a scavenger of party violence."[42] Sullivan's letter, on the other hand, was praised as speaking "the sentiments of the American people" and meriting "the warmest approbation."[43]

While Federalists and Republicans were still belaboring each other in this manner, John Quincy Adams entered the controversy with a public announcement which marked his final desertion of the Federalist cause and placed him definitely on the side of the administration. Always *persona non grata* with the high Federalists, he had been distrusted and disliked more than ever by New Englanders of the "Junto" persuasion since he had voted for the Embargo and had urged its passage on the ground that the President had "possessed such further information as authorized his recomending the measure."[44] Conscious

---

[40] *Interesting Correspondence between His Excellency Governor Sullivan and Col. Pickering* (Boston, 1808), Sullivan to Pickering, Mar. 18, 1808.

[41] *Salem Register*, Mar. 20, 1808, quoting resolutions of Plymouth Republicans.

[42] *Ibid.*, Apr. 2, 1808, quoting resolutions of Salem Republicans.

[43] *Ibid.*

[44] Pickering MSS., Pickering to Timothy Williams, Dec. 21, 1807. At this time Pickering described Adams' plea as "such a declaration of blind confidence as even a Democrat would be ashamed to express." The comment of Barent Gardiner, a New York Representative, was typical of the high Federalist attitude, "John Quincy Adams: His apostasy is no longer a matter of doubt with anybody . . . I wish to God that the noble house

of his position in the Federalist party, Adams believed that
the letter to Sullivan had been intended partly as a chal-
lenge to him and that, as one of the original supporters
of the Embargo, he was now bound to come to its defence.
Although the extreme Federalists had tried to win him
over to the anti-Embargo program, he had refused to join
them as he felt that the opposition measures proposed by
them were likely to lead to the dissolution of the Union.[45]
This opinion seemed to be confirmed by Pickering's letter,
which he saw as a dangerous document "with the avowed
purpose of stimulating the power of the separate states
to a resistance of force against the national government."[46]
If Pickering's appeal were successful, it would mean, too,
that the legislature which accepted its principles would
be bound to repudiate Adams when he came up for re-
election later in the year.   As a matter of fact, he was
convinced that that was precisely one of the objects at
which his colleague aimed in his effort to restore Massachusetts and the other northern states to Federalist control.[47]   Thus, considerations of both principle and policy
urged him to act in defence of the Union and of his own
political career.

Instead of answering Pickering directly, Adams attempted to accomplish his purpose by addressing a public
letter to Harrison Gray Otis, the leader of the Federalists
in the Massachusetts legislature.   This letter was at once
a condemnation of the principle of Pickering's appeal and
a refutation of his opinions of the causes of the Embargo.
Admitting that a state legislature had an undoubted right
to express its opinions on matters of national policy, he
argued that it should do so only after a careful consider-

of Braintree had been put in a hole and a deep one too twenty
years ago" (King, *Life and Correspondence of Rufus King*, V,
67-69, Gardiner to King, Jan. 26, 1808).

[45] Adams, *Memoirs of J. Q. Adams*, I, 510-11.

[46] Adams, *New England Federalism*, 195.

[47] W. C. Ford, *Writings of J. Q. Adams* (7 vols., New York,
1913-17), III, 232-35, J. Q. Adams to Abigail Adams, Apr. 20,
1808, "The letter of Pickering is another document of which I
could account for the origin from circumstances perhaps un-
known to you.   I was not named in the letter, but it was hardly
possible for me to avoid answering it."

ation of all sides of a question, and not on the basis of a partisan appeal. Otherwise, he could see no result but the destruction of the Union. Having disposed in this manner of the propriety of a Senator's appeal to his legislature, he went on to point out the falsity of the position Pickering had assumed in regard to the Embargo. He swept aside the allegation that Jefferson was under the influence of Napoleon, as he insisted that the aggressions of Great Britain had led the President to recommend the Embargo. It was the purpose of the British, he said, to reduce the United States to the position of a colony, a project in which he believed Pickering only too ready to assist. He could see no force whatever in his colleague's claim that Jefferson's reasons for urging the restrictive system upon Congress were only pretences, for he felt that the American grievances against England were very real and that the immediate cause of the Embargo was the Order in Council of November 11, even though it had not been mentioned in the executive message to Congress.[48]

Adams' letter was as complete a refutation of Pickering's appeal as any Republican could have asked; indeed it was a far more effective argument than Sullivan's answer had been. The Republicans, of course, were enormously pleased and they vied with each other, as their rivals said, to see who could praise Adams and abuse Pickering the more.[49] But able as the letter was, it came too late in the campaign to have any appreciable effect on the election.

Pickering's appeal to the Massachusetts electorate was by no means as successful as the Federalists had hoped, for the voters returned Governor Sullivan to office in the election held in the first week of April. The only possible causes for rejoicing were the reduction of the Republicans' popular majority and a Federalist victory in securing control of the state senate, indications that better times were in store for the minority party and that the

---

[48] Adams, *Letter to the Hon. Harrison Gray Otis . . . on the present state of our national affairs, with remarks upon Mr. Pickering's letter to the governor of Massachusetts* (Boston, 1808) ; Ford, *Writings of J. Q. Adams*, III, 189-223.

[49] *Salem Gazette*, Apr. 15, 1808.

anti-administration and anti-Embargo reaction had begun.[50] That this was the case was conclusively proved in a few weeks, when the election of the members of the lower house resulted in the choice of a Federalist majority of thirty.[51] By the time of the May election, then, it was quite apparent that the effects of the Embargo were more seriously felt in Massachusetts and that the Federalist agitation begun by Pickering was beginning to produce results.

The truth of the matter is that in the early months of the Embargo, that measure was not as unpopular as the Federalists wished it to be. Although its enemies represented it as producing immediate distress, its effects were not felt by all classes of the population until much later. As late as May, a Canadian observer reported that New England felt the Embargo less severely than New York, and that in Salem, where protests against the law had been extremely vociferous, there were no bankruptcies, although many merchants had on hand large stocks of goods which they could not sell.[52] Although there was little acute distress among the mass of the people, the merchant classes, who were socially and politically influential groups, were much affected by the loss of their profits from the war-time trade. As most of them naturally shared Pickering's political prejudices, they were only too ready to follow him in his attempt to organize discontent and distress into a party revolution. But in the early spring of 1808 there was not enough real suffering to make the Federalist appeal effective. Although the party leaders had hoped that Pickering's letter would arouse the people, they feared that public opinion at the

[50] *Ibid.*, June 3, 1808. The official vote for governor as announced at the opening of the legislature late in May was Sullivan, 41,502; Gore, 39, 823. In the state senate the Federalists had a majority of 23 to 17, but the decisive size of this majority occurred only because several of the regularly elected Republicans were unable to serve and the legislature chose Federalists to fill these vacancies. (King, *Life and Correspondence of Rufus King*, V, 98-99, Gore to King, May 28, 1808).

[51] King, *Life and Correspondence of Rufus King*, V, 98-99, Gore to King, May 28, 1808.

[52] *Am. Hist. Rev.*, XVII, 77-83, John Howe to Sir George Prevost, May 5. 1808.

time of the April election had not changed enough to defeat the Republicans, and in this they were correct.[53]

The enemies of Pickering and the high Federalists were convinced that the opposition to the Embargo was inspired by the British and that the purpose of the Federalists was to effect the secession of New England under the protection of Great Britain.[54] Although their belief was based mainly on circumstantial evidence and rumor, it was at least partially correct, for Pickering and the "Junto" were certainly working in conscious co-operation with the British government. Sullivan, who suspected the worst, was close to the truth when he wrote to Jefferson:

"I know not what Lyman your consul is about in England; Williams, his predecessor the Nephew of Pickering is very vigilant there. His letters give assurance to the merchants in England that the New England people will compel a repeal of the Embargo Act. His letters to his friends here give them assurance that great britain will cordially receive the returning northern states, and leave the Southern hemisphere to provide for its negroes, or to (sic) submit to the french for protection. You will stand astonished that any considerable portion of Massachusetts came forward in maintenance of such a project. But the old tories and old tory families (sic) are resuscitated: the aristocracy of wealth, even though nominal in banks, and wrapt in the base corruption of speculation has crowded all principle from our community, and our people are essentially changed. There are open and public avowals every day, in the assurance offices, that great britain is our only protector, that we are unable to protect ourselves, that her fleet is our fleet, her navy our navy, ..."[55]

From the very beginning of the controversy with the

[53] King, *Life and Correspondence of Rufus King*, V, 87-88, Gore to King, Mar. 10, 1808, "I have some hope that Pickering's letter, of which we shall distribute 5000 copies may arouse the people from their sleep, which appears like the sleep of death; but even of this I dare not predict."

[54] Adams, *New England Federalism*, 195-96; Jefferson MSS., Sullivan to Jefferson, Apr. 2, 5, 1808, quoted in Sears, *Jefferson and the Embargo*, 68-69.

[55] Jefferson MSS., Sullivan to Jefferson, Apr. 5, 1808, quoted in Sears, *Jefferson and the Embargo*, 69.

United States over the questions of neutral trade and
impressment, the British government had been interested
in using party and sectional discontent in America as a
means of defending British interests.   Its intention was
to encourage the hostility of the anti-administration forces
to Jefferson's measures without the necessity of going to
war, or, in the case of war, to attempt to arouse the northern states to open resistance to their national government.
At least one British secret agent in the United States had
suggested such policies to his government,[56] and Canadian
officials who were acquainted with the American situation represented New England as thoroughly hostile to
Jefferson and sympathetic with England.[57]   In England
the importance of the disaffection of the northern states
was fully appreciated[58] and the government was prepared
to turn it to advantage.[59]

Nothing could have been better suited to the purposes
of the British government in 1808 than the activities of
the high Federalists, of whom Pickering was the most
conspicuous figure then in public life.   When the British
minister, George H. Rose, came to the United States early
in the year to negotiate a settlement of the *Chesapeake*
affair, he was, to judge from his behavior, thoroughly
prepared to deal privately with Pickering and his group.
But willing as Rose undoubtedly was to treat with them,
they were far more willing, and even anxious, to impress

[56] The Williamson MSS. (Newberry Library, Chicago) contain
several letters of Charles Williamson, British secret agent in
the pre-Embargo period. Williamson frequently urged his government to "take advantage of the natural and strong disposition to internal division," (Williamson to [?], [Feb., 1805])
to encourage individuals opposed to the administration, (Williamson to the Lord Justice Clerk, June 5, 1807) and to conciliate New England and attach its citizens to the British interest (Williamson to Lord Melville, Nov. 15, 1807).

[57] *Am. Hist. Rev.*, XVII, 72, Sir John Wentworth to Castlereagh, Nov. 14, 1807.

[58] Charles Vane (ed.), *Memoirs and correspondence of Viscount
Castlereagh* (12 vols., London, 1848-52), VIII, 103-07, Castlereagh to Chatham, Dec. 31, 1807.

[59] *Am. Hist. Rev.*, XVII, 72-73, Castlereagh to Sir George Prevost, Feb. 13, 1808, "If this spirit be as general as we are led
to suppose, no means should be unemployed to take advantage
of it."

him with their friendship for Great Britain. Believing that there was little chance of reconciling Jefferson's policy with Rose's instructions, they were convinced that his mission would fail and feared that war with England would be the inevitable result.[60] To these Federalists there could be no greater disaster than such a war.[61] To avert that event, they hoped to persuade Rose that the purposes of Great Britain could be served without going to war if she would simply allow Jefferson to go ahead with his restrictive system until it should provoke a reaction significant enough to drive him from power or force him to modify his policy. At the same time, they wished to convince the minister that they would do all in their power to organize that reaction as the effective expression of the will of a popular minority willing to go to any lengths to defeat the administration.

After weeks of anxious waiting,[62] Pickering hastened to meet Rose as soon as he reached Washington. The senator was at once impressed with the friendly attitude of the envoy and, after their first meeting, he reported to King and Williams that he had already "formed a good opinion of him." He discovered, to his pleasure, that Rose was a close friend of Canning and that he possessed "good sense" and a "conciliatory disposition." "Our conversation was marked with ease and candour, indeed with singular openness as if I had been an old acquaintance," he wrote.[63]

With this auspicious beginning, Pickering set about to prove to Rose that there was in America an important

[60] King, *Life and Correspondence of Rufus King*, V, 46-50, Pickering to King, Jan. 2, 1808.

[61] Pickering MSS., King to Pickering, Dec. 31, 1807, "A war with England at this juncture is ruin to the Nation, and must be openly resisted"; Timothy Williams to Pickering, Feb. 12, 1808, "Is anything to save us from a war with England? The *virtue* and *wisdom* of ye people will not, no more than those of ye adminisn."

[62] Pickering MSS., Pickering to Williams, Dec. 24, 31, 1807; King, *Life and Correspondence of Rufus King*, V, 44-50, Pickering to King, Jan. 2, 1808 (two letters of same date).

[63] Pickering MSS., Pickering to Williams, Jan. 18, 1808; King, *Life and Correspondence of Rufus King*, V, 60-62, Pickering to King, Jan. 17, 1808.

party favorable to British interests, and that it would be
better policy for Great Britain to pursue a course of patience and forbearance than to assume an unyielding
attitude and force the United States into the war on the
side of France.

"I have taken the freedom to express earnestly to Mr. Rose
my opinion that good policy required on [Great Britain's]
part much patience and even long suffering, while we were
seriously punishing ourselves by the embargo,"

he wrote to King.[64] At the same time he asked Cabot
and King for their opinions and, finding that they agreed
with him, he added their pleas to his own.[65] As evidence
that he was himself active in the cause, he presented
Rose with a copy of his correspondence with Governor
Sullivan.[66]

Pickering's representations made a strong impression
upon Rose, who was so convinced of their worth that he
passed them along to Canning with favorable comments
of his own.[67] Of the effect which their conversations had
had upon the minister, Pickering was quite conscious, for
he told King:

"He has received my suggestions with great good will
and he manifests extreme anxiety for the amicable adjustment of our differences."[68]

Having succeeded then in convincing Rose of the existence
of a British party in America and having, in effect, concluded a sort of unofficial alliance with him, the senator
provided him with written proof of the policies and opin-

[64] King, *Life and Correspondence of Rufus King*, V, 83-85, Pickering to King, Mar. 4, 1808.

[65] *Ibid;* Lodge, *Cabot*, 386-89, Cabot to Pickering, Mar. 15, 1808,
". . . *the true policy of the British administration will be to
foil every attempt* to provoke them to put this country into
the hands of France"; Adams, *New England Federalism*, 366-67,
368-70, Pickering to Rose, Mar. 13, 22, 1808.

[66] Adams, *New England Federalism*, 368-70, Pickering to Rose,
Mar. 22, 1808.

[67] Adams, *History of the United States*, IV, 232-33, Rose to
Canning, Mar. 4, 1808, quoted from MSS., British Archives.

[68] King, *Life and Correspondence of Rufus King*, V, 83-85, Pickering to King, Mar. 4, 1808.

ions of the high Federalists in the form of two of his own letters, reinforced by the letters of Cabot and King. At the same time he suggested that they continue their negotiations through the medium of his nephew, Samuel Williams of London.[69] Thus equipped with documentary evidence, Rose set sail for England, but before he left he took the pains to compliment Pickering for his appeal to the Massachusetts legislature and to urge him "to go on letting in daylight and bidding the people 'awake'." Nor did he hesitate to tell him of his pleasure at receiving in the United States "the good will of one of her truest patriots and most distinguished citizens, to have conciliated whose good opinion has been one of the most consoling circumstances of my unavailing expedition."[70] Back in London a few weeks later, Rose reported to the government and labored to convince it and the British public that in America there existed a strong party favorable to their interests. As a proof, Rose, or some other,[71] gave Pickering's letter to Sullivan to the press and it was reprinted for the benefit of English readers. It was so well received by them that Rose could write to his American friend:

"Your modesty would suffer if you were aware of the sensation produced in this country by the publication of a letter from a senator of Massachusetts to his constituents."[72]

But Rose was not the only representative from whom the British government learned of the work of the Federalist leaders, for during the spring of 1808 two secret agents from Canada endeavored to ascertain the strength and real purposes of the anti-administration party. From Montreal came John Henry, an unofficial observer, who

[69] Adams, *New England Federalism*, 366-67, 368-70, Pickering to Rose, Mar. 13, 22, 1808.

[70] *Ibid.*, 367-68, 370-71, Rose to Pickering, Mar. 18, 23, 1808.

[71] It might have come from any one of several sources, for the letter was so generally published in America and so quickly recognized as something of value to the English cause that many copies found their way to Canada and thence to England. Both John Henry and John Howe obtained copies and sent them to Canada.

[72] Adams, *New England Federalism*, 371-72, Rose to Pickering, May 8, 1808.

had once lived in Boston and who now tried to make himself useful to Sir James Craig, the governor-general of
Lower Canada, by sending him reports of conditions as
he found them in New England, while from Halifax
came John Howe, a former Boston Loyalist, sent by Sir
George Prevost to learn what he could of the political
situation in the United States. Although neither one
established any direct connection with Pickering, both
learned from general observation and from their contacts
with Federalist friends much the same information that
Pickering had given to Rose. Both men read Pickering's letter to Sullivan and, believing that it would assist
the anti-Embargo reaction, sent copies of it to their supe-
riors with approving comments. Both men saw that the
Federalists were growing stronger in the northern states
and both recommended in substance what Pickering had
urged upon Rose, that the British government bide its
time in dealing with the United States and refuse either
to make any concessions or to go to war, for, in their
opinion, the growing discontent in the north would soon
force the administration to abandon its policy. Henry,
indeed, reported that there was talk of organized resistance to the measures of the national government and
that plans were already being laid to bring about the secession of the northern states in case Jefferson's obnoxious
policies should be carried further and war with England
should result. In arriving at that opinion he was probably deceived by the strong talk of many Federalists and
in all likelihood he erroneously took the Massachusetts
Federalist machine to be a seditious organization of committees of correspondence. But no matter how much
Henry or Howe might err in details, their general obser-
vations on the state of public opinion were substantially
correct and their reports tended to corroborate what Pickering had told to Rose, as they gave the impression of a
pro-British Federalist party, constantly increasing in
strength and determination to adopt the most extreme
measures against its opponents.[73]

[73] *Report on the Canadian Archives (1893): State Papers,
Lower Canada, Calendar, 1808-13* (Douglas Brymner, ed., Ottawa,

Although the Embargo and the Federalists' vigorous denunciation of it did not create an immediate reaction to Jefferson in New England, there were many signs that a movement was beginning there and that it was gathering strength. Among the first of such signs were the memorials adopted by many town-meetings and Federalist gatherings in Massachusetts to petition Congress to remove the Embargo. In most cases these petitions were relatively mild, merely stating that the law had had disastrous effects and requesting the government to remove it, and they did not make the suggestions of radical opposition that appeared a few months later.[74] These protests, however, proved unavailing and soon an entirely different type of opposition appeared, when the Federalist legislature in its first session after the spring election of 1808 passed a resolution condemning the Embargo and declaring its belief that a permanent law of that nature was unconstitutional. Although this resolution was introduced by Laban Wheaton, an obscure representative from Norton, it was supposed to have been written by Christopher Gore, the defeated Federalist candidate for governor, who accepted the views of the most extreme wing of his party. The Republicans, led by Joseph Story, worked hard to defeat it, but could not succeed against the overwhelming Federalist majority.[75]

At the same session the Federalist majority took its vengeance on John Quincy Adams for his "apostasy" in supporting Sullivan and the Embargo. Federalists could not believe that his course had been prompted by anything but the meanest ambition, the hope of reward from the

---

1894), 5-9, for the Henry letters of 1808; "Secret Reports of John Howe, 1808," *Am. Hist. Rev.*, XVII, 70-112, 332-54 (David W. Parker, ed.).

[74] Sears, *Jefferson and the Embargo*, 152-53, quoting and listing the petitions preserved in the Jefferson MSS.

[75] John S. Barry, *The History of Massachusetts* (3 vols., Boston, 1857), III, 359-60; W. W. Story, *Life and Letters of Joseph Story* (2 vols., Boston, 1851), I, 136-38.

Republican administration.[76] For daring to oppose their leader, the Federalists now drove Adams from the party and forced him to resign his seat in the Senate, as they elected his successor, contrary to the usual custom, nearly a year before his term expired. To take his place, they immediately chose James Lloyd, a Boston Federalist in good standing, who could be relied upon to vote with Pickering on all questions.[77] Adams, of course, was much embittered by this event, although he had expected to feel the full weight of Federalist disapproval. Yet he must have found some solace in his appointment as minister to Russia, which came a few months later from the grateful Republicans.[78] To Pickering, however, the legislature's rejection of Adams was highly gratifying, for it marked the victorious conclusion of another chapter in his feud with the Adams family, though it did not lessen his hatred for either the father or the son.[79] Furthermore,

[76] A typical high Federalist opinion of Adams is that of Timothy Williams (Pickering MSS., Apr. 11, 1808), "Who knows that he is not on some fair and delusive promises, hired or tempted to put his shoulder to ye wheel of Gover't, sinking so fast and deep in mire and difficulty! What his father would do to gratify a malignant party by sacrificing you as an illustrious victim; would ye son, even less humane and social, hesitate to do, goaded by proud envy and young ambition?"

[77] Adams, *Memoirs*, I, 535-36; W. C. Ford, "The Recall of John Quincy Adams in 1808," *Mass. Hist. Soc. Proc.*, XLV, 354-75.

[78] As early as April, two months before his expulsion from the Senate, Adams learned that the Republicans were anxious to appoint him to office and that they would do so soon if he would indicate in his public writings his support of their constitutional principles. With his customary independence, he refused to make such a bid for office. (Adams, *Memoirs*, I, 532-33.)

[79] Pickering had considered writing a public letter in answer to Adams' *Letter to Otis*, but he seems to have dropped the project after Adams' defeat in the legislature. Yet he and his friends continued to abuse the Adamses on every possible occasion (Bentley, *Diary*, III, 372.) A few months later, however, some further work of Adams in support of the Republicans aroused Pickering's passion and again he considered writing a denunciation of the family. When it was rumored that the Adamses would expose his intrigues as Secretary of State and charge him with having suppressed certain despatches, he was thrown into a rage and wrote to Timothy Williams (Pickering MSS., Feb. 4, 1809), "If the A—s dare to offer that pretence publicly, I shall not spare the Old Man. Hitherto I have said as little as possible *for the sake of his federal friends* & the *federal cause* of which he was once the official head."

this victory and the passage of Wheaton's anti-Embargo resolution placed the unmistakable mark of the legislature's approval upon the principles and program he had set forth in the letter to Sullivan.

Among the Federalists Pickering became a hero. Upon his return from Washington at the close of the session of Congress, he was hailed as the leader of the party and the defender of its principles. `In Salem the members of the party planned to honor him publicly and they invited several Boston Federalists to join with them. Consequently, on May 24, he was entertained as the guest of honor at a great celebration. On the morning of that day a cavalcade of one hundred young men, the pride of local Federalism, met him at the Wenham line as he came from his home to Salem. From that point the triumphal procession passed through Beverly, across Northfield Bridge, where the ships in Beverly harbor saluted him, and into Salem to Concert Hall, where the banquet was held. There, with Benjamin Goodhue as the presiding officer and Josiah Quincy as the principal speaker, the Federalists held a fitting celebration, with toasts that damned Jefferson and the Embargo as they praised Pickering and the commercial interests of which he was the great defender. Yet not all of Salem rejoiced at Timothy's homecoming, for the Republicans were still numerous and noisy, and they took the occasion to express their disapproval of the Senator and his conduct by hanging him in effigy and publicly burning copies of the letter to Sullivan, while on the Marblehead side of the harbor the Republicans of that town hanged an effigy sardonically labelled "The Hero of Lexington" and holding the "Letter to Sullivan" in its right hand. Parson Bentley was so angered by the Federalist celebration that he left the town in disgust to spend the day at Nahant, in marked contrast to most of his fellow-clergymen, who were conspicuous figures in the group that gathered at Concert Hall. Bentley, indeed, described the whole affair as "an insult to our government," and there were many who agreed with him. On the other hand, it was the Feder-

alist opinion that the Republican demonstration was a
"poor, sneaking, dirty, malicious transaction."[80]

While there were these evidences of Pickering's growing
popularity and of the increasing acceptance of his principles, there was as yet no conclusive proof that the majority of the people were ready to accept his suggestion
of radical opposition, even though it might be approved
by most of the outstanding Federalist leaders, such as
Cabot and Gore. On the contrary, the Republicans remained strong and active. Their papers never lost an
opportunity to denounce the Federalists and vilify Pickering,[81] while their party gatherings on holiday occasions
indulged themselves in the expression of extreme opinions
which ranked Pickering with Aaron Burr.[82] More important, however, was the fact that Republicans still held
the executive branch of the state government, and were
thus in a position to block or delay any radical Federalist
action. Both Governor Sullivan and the Lieutenant-
Governor, Levi Lincoln, were thoroughly suspicious of
their opponents' purposes and were consequently watchful
of every move.[83] Sullivan was convinced that the Federalists aimed at secession and he feared their success so
much that he urged Jefferson not to enforce the law rigidly
in New England. Lincoln, however, believed that there

[80] *Salem Gazette*, May 24, 27, 1808; Bentley, *Diary*, III, 361-62.
[81] For example, see the *Salem Register* (June 4, 1808) on the
occasion of the defeat of Adams and the election of Lloyd, "It
is astonishing to what lengths the federal party will go in
opposition to the government, . . . We blush for the honor
of the Commonwealth." From time to time the same paper
attacked Pickering on the ground that he was a servant of
Great Britain and among other things cited as proof his delay
at the battle of Lexington and the story that he, while Secretary of State, had received a pension from Robert Liston. A
comment in the *Boston Democrat* (quoted in the *Newburyport
Herald*, May 27, 1808) is also typical, "What Timothy lacks in
talent, he makes up in impudence. — His reputation is too low
for him to do Republicanism any harm."
[82] *Salem Gazette*, July 8, 1808, quoting a Republican toast of
July 4, "The Pickerings and Burrs of the United States: May
the people be aware they have internal enemies."
[83] The Jefferson MSS. contain many letters from Sullivan and
Lincoln during 1808 which constantly warned the President of
the state of affairs in Massachusetts. Many of them are quoted
rather fully in Sears, *Jefferson and the Embargo*.

was more smoke than fire and felt that the Republicans could handle the situation by conducting a more vigorous campaign in their own defense.

Under such circumstances it was clearly inadvisable for the Federalists to take any steps toward the nullification of the Embargo, although, to judge from their acts and utterances, that was their evident purpose, if all other measures failed. Hence, they found it necessary to devote themselves to whipping-up the anti-Embargo sentiment and to laying plans for the national election in the fall. Hoping to insure the choice of Federalist electors in Massachusetts, they planned to have the electors chosen by the legislature, where the Federalist majority was certain. Realizing, however, that Sullivan would try to block this move, they decided to postpone action from the June session until November, and even then it was necessary to adopt that method by a legislative order rather than by a resolution which would require the executive signature. Although the Republicans condemned this proceeding as unconstitutional, the Federalist majority had its way.[84] At the same time the Massachusetts Federalists joined with their fellow partisans from other states to decide upon one presidential candidate who could be supported by all. At an informal meeting in New York in August, a handful of Federalist leaders, representative not of the rank and file of the party, but only of its inner circles, decided to unite their followers in support of C. C. Pinckney and Rufus King.[85] This step seemed wise to Pickering and he commended it, but took care to point out that the party might not be strong enough to elect its candidates, and that in that case it ought to unite with the anti-Jeffersonian wing of the Republicans to give its votes to "a northern Democrat, of practical talents, of

[84] King, *Life and Correspondence of Rufus King*, V, 100-01, Gore to King, June 8, 1808; T. C. Amory, *Life of James Sullivan* (2 vols., Boston, 1859), II, 311-12; Ford, *Writings of J. Q. Adams*, III, 248-53, Adams to Ezekiel Bacon, Nov. 17, 1808. Adams and Sullivan were clearly of the opinion that this method was unconstitutional. Adams, too, believed that it was another step in provoking a clash between state and national authority.

[85] S. E. Morison, "The First National Nominating Convention, 1808," *Am. Hist. Rev.*, XVII, 744-63; Morison, *Otis*, I, 304-08.

energy of character, & a friend to commerce."[86]   In view of the frequent statement that Pickering was a secessionist in 1808, this advice assumes some importance, for it places him as one whose real interest was the practical one of restoring the lost influence of Federalism within the Union.   It was apparently his hope to defeat Jefferson's Embargo by combining with the moderate Republicans who were friendly to the commercial interests, if that seemed to be the most practical method.

But even while placing such emphasis on the coming election, Pickering and his friends did not neglect other modes of action, and they kept before their section and the nation at large the threat of nullification.   Following the example of the Boston town-meeting of August 9, towns throughout Massachusetts adopted petitions to the President, praying that the Embargo be entirely or partially suspended.   Four months earlier, these towns had petitioned Congress for relief, but they now turned to the President, as Congress had invested him with discretionary power to suspend or modify the law.[87]   In this form of protest, too, Pickering was active, for he led his town of Wenham in the adoption of a petition which emphasized the depression of agriculture as a result of the Embargo.[88]   Yet even this kind of protest was far from being unanimously supported, for many communities, including Salem and Marblehead, refused to take such action and, instead, some of them voted resolutions approving the policy of the administration.[89]   In Salem the Federalists tried for two months to secure a town-meeting which would vote an anti-Embargo resolution, but when a meeting was finally called in October, the prestige of William Gray and the eloquence of Joseph Story defeated the project.[90]   Gray incidentally had become a Republican and a supporter of the Embargo only a few weeks

[86] Pickering MSS., Pickering to Killian K. Van Rensselaer, Sept. 26, 1808.

[87] Morison, *Otis*, I, 330-31.

[88] *Salem Gazette*, Aug. 19, 1808; Bentley, *Diary*, III, 377-78.

[89] *Salem Gazette*, Aug. 30, Sept. 16, Sept. 22, Oct. 11, 1808; Bentley, *Diary*, III, 377-78.

[90] *Salem Gazette*, Oct. 28, 1808; Bentley, *Diary*, III, 391-92.

earlier, and as he was the richest merchant of the town, his conversion was reckoned a great gain to Republicanism.[91] The Federalists, of course, denounced him for his "apostasy," and ranked him with John Quincy Adams. Pickering, through his son, John, and Stephen Higginson, Jr., worked hard to discredit him by charging that his shift of opinion was dictated by pecuniary motives, but their attack was not convincing.[92]

Jefferson, of course, was unmoved by these petitions and, failing in this type of attack, the Federalists turned to more radical measures. The opinion stated in Wheaton's resolution that the Embargo was unconstitutional was a common one and an attempt was made to have the law set aside on that ground. When tried in September before Judge John Davis at a session of the Federal District Court in Salem, the attempt failed, but the arguments of the counsel gave strength and publicity to the Federalist cause.[93] Unfortunately for the extremists, there seemed to be no way of bringing such a case before the state courts, where Theophilus Parsons and his fellow judges would have been quite willing to test their strength against the national government.[94] During this same period much talk of the secession of New England arose. It soon became prominent in the Federalist press and was heard in the pulpits of the orthodox clergy, who hated anything tinged with Jeffersonianism.[95] When the Republicans began to protest against the proposals of secession, the editor of the Federalist *Salem Gazette* replied by asking:

[91] Bentley, *Diary*, III, 364.

[92] *Salem Gazette*, Aug. 5, Aug. 12, 1808; Bentley, *Diary*, III, 376-77; Pickering MSS., Correspondence of John Pickering, Jr., Stephen Higginson, Jr., William Gray, and T. C. Cushing, editor of the *Salem Gazette*, Aug. 3–Oct. 10, 1808.

[93] Adams, *History of the United States*, IV, 268; Amory, *Sullivan*, II, 306; Bentley, *Diary*, III, 384-85.

[94] Adams, *New England Federalism*, 222-24.

[95] *Columbian Centinel*, Sept. 10-24, 1808; *Salem Gazette*, Sept. 27–Oct. 11, 1808; *Thomas Jefferson Correspondence* (Printed from the originals in the collection of William K. Bixby, W. C. Ford, ed.), 170-71, Elisha Tracy to Jefferson, Sept. 15, 1808; *Am. Hist. Rev.*, XVII, 332-34, Howe to Prevost, Sept., 1808.

"What charms can a *union* have for New England, if all her commerce by land and water, and all the sources of her prosperity and greatness, must be sacrificed? She wishes to preserve the Union, she wishes also to preserve her own rights."[96]

But in spite of such public declarations, secession was not then the aim of the little group of leaders who formulated the policies of Federalism. In fact, George Cabot believed that these announcements would do more harm than good, for they would prevent many moderate men from voting Federalist in November and would provide the Republicans with some proof for their charges that their opponents were seditious. With that in mind, he suggested to Pickering that it would be wise to sponsor the adoption of "some very decided resolution on the importance of maintaining the Union inviolable under every trial."[97] A similar idea must have been in the minds of many prominent Federalists that fall, for the county conventions of the party carefully avoided any recommendation of disunion, although they condemned the Embargo more vigorously than ever. In the Essex County Convention at Topsfield, in which Pickering was influential, although not officially a member, a resolution was adopted which clearly outlined the program of Massachusetts Federalism in case the national election should not result favorably and in case the Republican administration should consistently refuse to modify its policy. In a word, it was nullification, and declared:

"We firmly rely for relief on the wisdom and patriotism of our STATE GOVERNMENT, whom the people have placed as sentinels to guard our rights and privileges, from whatever quarter they may be invaded. We trust that *they* will take care that the Constitution of the United States be maintained in its spirit as well as in its letter."[98]

Though the authorship of this resolution cannot be definitely ascribed to Pickering, his influence is unmistak-

[96] *Salem Gazette*, Sept. 27, 1808.

[97] Adams, *New England Federalism*, 373, Cabot to Pickering, Oct. 5, 1808.

[98] *Salem Gazette*, Oct. 14, 1808; *Columbian Centinel*, Oct. 12, 1808; Bentley, *Diary*, III, 389.

able, for it closely resembles his position in the letter to Sullivan and his attitude during the events of the subsequent winter.

Soon it became clear that this was the program of the Massachusetts Federalists, for the November election did not produce a national Federalist reaction, although it did completely "federalize" New England and thus insure the party of support in that section. In the Essex South District, the Federalists won a notable victory that, as Samuel Putnam told his chief, "ought to give great joy to Federalists in every part of the Union,"[99] for a Federalist carried the district for the first time since Jacob Crowninshield had defeated Pickering in 1802. There Benjamin Pickman, Jr., triumphed over Daniel Kilham, a little known Republican, in spite of all the efforts of the Crowninshields and Joseph Story to defend the administration.[100] In New England this victory was especially significant, for Pickman was a close friend and political ally of Pickering, while the vote might be correctly interpreted as an endorsement of the Topsfield Resolution.

In the meantime Pickering had started for Washington, where he would be ready to open a new attack on the administration and the Embargo. Altogether his position was much improved over that of the previous spring, when he had been nearly helpless. His new colleague, Lloyd, was sure to support him; the election results were encouraging; and the growth of the opposition in New England, he felt, had "excited great uneasiness in the breasts of the administration."[101] Under the circumstances, it seemed wise to press for the immediate repeal of the Embargo. Consequently his friend, Hillhouse of Connecticut, presented a resolution to appoint a committee to prepare a bill for repeal, while Lloyd demanded an investigation of the exceptions to the enforcement of the law allowed to friends of the administration.[102] Their purpose was shortly encouraged by a resolution of the Massachusetts

99 Pickering MSS., Putnam to Pickering, Nov. 9, 1808.
100 *Ibid.; Salem Gazette*, Nov. 8, 1808; Bentley, *Diary*, III, 395.
101 King, *Life and Correspondence of Rufus King*, V, 107-08, Pickering to King, Nov. 19, 1808.
102 *Annals of Congress*, 10th, 2nd, 16.

legislature instructing its Senators to work for immediate repeal.[103] Fittingly enough, in view of his earlier appeal to the legislature, Pickering now presented the resolution to the Senate and succeeded in having it read into the record, in spite of an opposition which declared that a legislature had no right to instruct its Senators.[104]

When Hillhouse's resolution for repeal came up for discussion, Pickering was foremost in debate. His arguments were mainly the ones that he had used before. In the course of a long and rambling speech, he elaborated, perhaps unintentionally, on what had come to be the two major articles of his political creed: a prejudice in favor of Great Britain as against France and an unswerving devotion to the interests of maritime commerce. He repeated his contention that the Embargo was the result of French influence and not of British aggressions. In support of this claim he offered again the account of the passage of the Embargo that had appeared in his letter to Sullivan and he flatly denied that the Order in Council of November 11 could be considered a cause. Furthermore, he insisted that Great Britain had by no means violated American rights so clearly and indisputably as to justify either embargo or war. He pointed out that the restrictive system was irreparably ruining American foreign commerce and asserted that if the law were not in force the nation's foreign trade would at that moment be enjoying a prosperity unequalled in times of peace, in spite of all the British and French raids on neutral shipping. To prove his assertions he quoted the opinions of eminent Massachusetts merchants and the statistics furnished by the maritime insurance houses. He realized, he said, that his attack on the Embargo laid him open to the charge that he was a Tory and a recipient of British gold, and he answered his critics by accusing them of demagoguery and deliberate falsification to support themselves and their policies. Referring to the talk of secession in New England and to Republican criticism of it, he defended his native section by comparing the oppression

---

[103] *Ibid.*, 129-31; *Salem Gazette*, Nov. 22, 1808.
[104] *Annals of Congress*, 10th, 2nd, 127-31.

of the commercial states under the Embargo to that of the pre-Revolutionary era, which, as he commented rather significantly, was universally considered a just and sufficient cause of revolution. Finally, he called attention to the fact that the Embargo had not fulfilled its purpose, as both belligerent nations still clung to their original policies. Hence, he concluded that the law ought to be repealed immediately and he utterly repudiated Jefferson's position that it could not be repealed without loss of honor until Great Britain modified her orders in council, for he could see no connection between the two measures when, as he believed, the Order of November 11 had not been a cause of the Embargo.[105]

But the Senate was unimpressed. Although Lloyd and Hillhouse joined Pickering in the argument for repeal, they found few supporters. Apparently most of the Senators agreed with Giles of Virginia, an administration spokesman, who denounced Pickering and declared:

"The gentleman seems to be still harping on the miserable tale of French influence, . . . Sir, insinuations of this nature are degrading to the national character; and I always feel a condescension in being compelled to make a reply. . . .

"I will not accuse this gentleman of acting under British influence; I feel too much respect for the American character to do so. I hope and trust he is not. I am willing to admit that his views are American. But, sir, this consideration will not deter me from expressing my wonder and astonishment at the extraordinary views the gentleman takes of American interests; first in the unremitting labor he has taken to put his own government in the wrong upon every point of discussion between it and the British Government; and in his strange misrepresentation or total disregard of facts; of outrages, sir, upon our dearest rights, by the British Government, outrages which ought to rouse every American feeling into action. Secondly, in the comparative view he has taken of the hostile acts of France and Great Britain. Sir, he has used every effort to magnify, if possible, French aggressions; whilst he has faintly admitted British aggressions, and even palliated or excused them."[106]

[105] *Annals of Congress*, 10th, 2nd, 175-94.
[106] *Ibid.*, 212-29.

When the final vote was taken, only six Senators supported the resolution for repeal.[107]   Not a single Republican was won over by Pickering and Hillhouse.

Instead of yielding any part of the restrictive system, the Republicans now undertook to make its operation more effective by passing a new and stringent enforcing act.[108] Pickering, of course, opposed the measure most vociferously and took the occasion to give his political views a further airing. He proposed indirectly that the best thing for the United States to do would be to repeal the Embargo, come to terms with England, and join her in attacking France as the common enemy of civilization.[109] But again he received the support of only a small Federalist minority.[110]

The failure of these frontal attacks on the administration gave evidence of Jefferson's determination to keep the Embargo if possible and convinced Pickering that the time had come for more radical action.   He believed that the Embargo was being maintained "only to save the reputation of its authors,[111] and that the President *would rather the United States should sink than change the present system of measures.*"[112] For a time he considered writing an extended review of Jefferson's administration for the purpose of exposing what he believed to be its wicked policies,[113] but he soon abandoned this plan.[114] Even while he was planning this attack and gathering information for it, other lines of action were proving more profitable.   All New England was swinging over to

107 *Ibid.*, 230.

108 *Annals of Congress*, 10th, 2nd, 298.

109 *Ibid.*, 276-82.

110 *Ibid.*, 298.

111 Pickering MSS., Pickering to David Parish, Dec. 8, 1808; to John Jay, Dec. 10, 1808.

112 Adams, *New England Federalism,* 376-78, 379-80, Pickering to Gore, Jan. 8, 1809; Pickering to S. P. Gardner [Feb., 1809]; King, *Life and Correspondence of Rufus King,* V, 133, Pickering to King, Feb. 2, 1809; Pickering MSS., Pickering to Timothy Williams, Feb. 4, 1809.

113 Pickering MSS., Pickering to S. P. Gardner, Jan. 10, 1809; to John Jay, Jan. 13, 1809; to Timothy Williams, Feb. 4, 1809; to John Smith, Feb. 12, 1809.

114 *Ibid.*, Pickering to John Jay, Feb. 23, 1809.

his side and by January it was apparent that the Massachusetts legislature, angered by the Senate's treatment of its resolution and encouraged by the rise of popular discontent, would during its winter session take some action in line with what Pickering had been suggesting for months. Now he could see that more was to be gained from directing the resistance of Massachusetts than from following any other plan of attack.

New England was now seething with discontent. As winter set in, the economic distress of large numbers became acute, as even that devoted partisan of Jefferson, the Reverend William Bentley, had to admit as he recorded the activities of charity in Salem.[115] Although the seaports were the chief sufferers, the rural districts were also affected. As this distress grew, Jefferson's policies became more distasteful than ever and talk of armed resistance, and even of secession, became common. So loud was this rumble of discontent that in December John Howe, the Canadian observer, wrote to a friend:

"If the present oppressive system of Embargo or nonintercourse is persisted in, and our Government should not think it good policy to help them out of their present embarrassed situation, it is highly probable that a separation of these States will be the consequence. — That indignation against the measures of their Government, which I noticed when I passed through New England, in the Summer, has now arisen to a much greater height, and as I passed through now on my way to Washington, I became fully satisfied that the Inhabitants of the Southern States [of New England] will not much longer suffer themselves to be excluded from the ocean."[116]

Of this temper of the people Pickering was duly informed by his many correspondents.[117]

Such news served to strengthen his convictions, and

[115] Bentley, *Diary*, III, 413.

[116] Canadian Archives MSS., John Howe to Francis Freeling, Dec. 9, 1808.

[117] Pickering MSS., Rev Justus Forward (of Belchertown) to Pickering, Dec. 9, 1808, Jan. 25, 1809; Rev. Manasseh Cutler to Pickering, Dec. 28, 1808, Jan. 5, 1809; Israel Thorndike to Pickering, Dec. 31, 1808.

when Christopher Gore wrote on December 20 to ask what course the legislature should pursue at its winter session, and to suggest that it should step cautiously unless several other states should show some willingness to co-operate with Massachusetts in concerting measures of opposition,[118] Pickering, although seeming to agree on the necessity for the united action of all the New England states, recommended nullification.

"Pray look into the Constitution," he wrote, "particularly to the tenth article of the amendments. How are powers reserved to the States respectively, or to the people, to be maintained, *but by the respective states judging for themselves & putting their negative on the usurpations of the general government.*"[119]

But whatever hesitation he may have had vanished in the course of the next few weeks, as town meetings all over Massachusetts besought the legislature to act in their defense. Their resolutions summarized the grievances of the discontented groups and declared, "No resource remains to us but in the protection of our State Legislature."[120] At last the reaction for which Pickering had hoped had come and affairs had come to such a pass that it was necessary for the legislature to take some action. Just what that action should be was the question that bothered the Federalist leaders of Massachusetts. Pickering, however, did not share the doubts of most of his associates. In Washington he had observed that, in spite of much discussion of a change in the administration policy, Jefferson was still determined to maintain the Embargo, or at least to postpone the date of repeal until he was out of office. Hence, Pickering concluded that the

[118] Adams, *New England Federalism*, 375-76.

[119] *Ibid.*, 376-78, Pickering to Gore, Jan. 9, 1809.

[120] *Salem Gazette*, Jan. 27, 1809, quoting the resolution of the Boston town meeting of Jan. 23. Instances of such petitions may be seen in nearly every issue of the Massachusetts newspapers during January and February, 1809. Their content is effectively summarized in "The Report of the Joint Committee on Petitions" printed in *The Patriotick Proceedings of the Legislature of Massachusetts, during their session from Jan. 26 to Mar. 4, 1809*, (Boston, 1809).

time had come to strike, and strike hard, in order that the President might be forced to yield at once.

While in this state of mind, he wrote to Timothy Williams on February 4:

"Upon this aspect of things, it behooves our state legislature to advance with a firm step, in defense of the rights of our citizens and of the Constitution. The least relaxation or wavering in the Councils of N. England would give them fresh courage, & hazard the most disastrous consequences."[121]

In even more forceful terms he replied to one request for advice,[122] that he hoped that the counsel of timid men would not prevail in Massachusetts.

"Defeat the accursed measure now," he demanded, "and you not only restore commerce, agriculture, and all sorts of business to activity, but save the country from a British war. The power of the present miserable rulers will then be annihilated. It is only for Massachusetts and Connecticut, or even Massachusetts alone, to will the defeat of the Embargo Acts and they will become a dead letter. But if there be wavering and timidity—our worst enemies—the devoted adherents of France will rise with renewed and increased force and assuredly plunge this country into a war with Great Britain."[123]

But few other Federalist leaders were willing to take such a bold and emphatic stand in favor of nullification as Pickering, although they were equally desirous of driving Jefferson from his adherence to the Embargo. Some of them felt that the Union was in danger and they did not care to precipitate disunion by a hasty step toward nullification. A few, indeed, endeavored to impress Pickering with their fears.[124] To at least one of them Picker-

121 Pickering MSS., Pickering to Timothy Williams, Feb. 4, 1809.

122 Adams, *New England Federalism*, 378-79, Samuel Blanchard to Pickering, Jan. 16, 1809. Blanchard, one of Pickering's Essex County followers, asked that the Senator send his advice to S. P. Gardner of Boston.

123 *Ibid.*, 379-80, Pickering to S. P. Gardner [Feb., 1809].

124 Pickering MSS., William Rawle to Pickering, Nov. 23, 1808, "The greatest evil that in the present critical state of our affairs could possibly happen would be an attempt at separation —Embargo, non-intercourse, or foreign war tho' oppressive are

ing gave assurance that his plans did not involve a severance of the bonds of union.[125] Apparently he felt that the issue would never be pushed that far. In fact, an examination of his correspondence gives the distinct impression that he believed that even nullification would not be put to the test completely, for he expected Jefferson to quail before the determined stand of the Massachusetts legislature.

But the advices of the moderate men prevailed, for the Massachusetts legislature stopped short of actual nullification. In what the Federalists were pleased to style "The Patriotick Proceedings," the legislature justified the appeals of the town meetings, condemned the Embargo, gave its opinion that the law was unconstitutional, drew up a remonstrance to Congress, published an address to the people of the state, and called upon the other commercial states to join Massachusetts in proposing constitutional amendments to safeguard their interests. But it was notable that while the legislature went so far, it did not declare the law null and void and it did ask the people to refrain from forcible resistance. Its only positive action was to issue a call for a convention of the commercial states to decide what measures were necessary to protect their interests.[126]

---

less to be dreaded — Fervently do I hope that their dissatisfaction will stop short of this extreme point—the dissolution of the Union"; Noah Webster to Pickering, Dec. 17, 1808, "I hope the opposers of Mr. Jefferson's plans & measures will be tranquil—& leave the *measures* to have their natural effect upon the public. Passions are increased & opposition rendered more violent & fixed by a collision of opinions. The federalists will do all they can to arrest the progress of bad measures in transition, but I think they had better be moderate in their opposition to them when passed. Such measures *must* in *time* work a cure. The evils we must suffer will be beyond calculation, but we had better submit to them, than not to be cured." Cf. similar protests in Adams, *New England Federalism*, 380-81, Richard Peters to Pickering, Feb. 3, 1809.

[125] Adams, *New England Federalism*, 380-81, Richard Peters to Pickering, Feb. 3, 1809, mentions a letter from Pickering assuring Peters of the safety of the Union.

[126] *The Patriotick Proceedings of the Legislature of Massachusetts* (Boston, 1809). The more essential portions of these *Proceedings* are printed in H. V. Ames, *State Documents on Federal Relations* (Philadelphia, 1906), I, 26-33.

While these measures were undoubtedly less emphatic and radical than Pickering had desired, he had to be content with them. At least part of his purpose was accomplished, for already all of New England but New Hampshire had returned to Federalist leadership, and on March 1 the Embargo was replaced by Non-Intercourse. For that concession on the part of the Jefferson administration, the protest movement in which Pickering had played such a conspicuous part was in large measure responsible. Its success in winning the support of thousands and its frequent discussion and threat of secession had alarmed many northern Republicans like Joseph Story, until these men were convinced that the only safety for the nation and their party lay in a modification of the administration policy.[127] Even Jefferson admitted that the northern opposition was a major cause of his defeat. He, too, feared that disunion was approaching and that the real object of the Massachusetts Federalists was "to take advantage of the first war with England to separate the N. E. states from the union."[128] Bitter at his failure to ruin the "Essex Junto," an object dear to his heart, he complained of the defection of the northern members of his party and blamed them for the surrender to Federalism,[129] but at the same time he recognized that the acts of the Massachusetts towns and the "Patriotick Proceedings" of the state legislature were fundamentally responsible for his defeat.[130]

For the defeat of the Embargo and the revival of New England Federalism, Pickering was probably more responsible than any other one man. From the first he saw the opportunity which was presented to his party. He de-

[127] Ford, *Writings of J. Q. Adams*, III, 260-67, 272-75; Story, *Life of Joseph Story*, I, 174-75, 177-87, 190-92.

[128] Jefferson, *Works*, IX, 236-37, Jefferson to William Eustis, Oct. 6, 1809.

[129] *Ibid.*, 276, Jefferson to Henry Dearborn, July 16, 1810.

[130] Morison, *Otis*, II, 14, quoting Jefferson MSS., "I felt the foundation of the government shaken under my feet by the New England townships"; Jefferson, *Works*, IX, 276-78, Jefferson to Judge John Tyler, May 26, 1810, ". . . by them the Eastern States were enabled to repeal the Embargo in opposition to the Middle, Southern, and Western States, . . ."

veloped the political and economic argument against Jefferson's pacific policy and indicated the method by which the commercial states might defeat it. His appeal to his constituents accelerated the Federalist reaction of 1808 and his voice was prominent in the party councils that carried that reaction to at least a partial victory. Although his program was not completely accepted, in all likelihood a union of the commercial states would have nullified the Embargo if the repeal of the law had not intervened. In assuming the leadership of the opposition to Jefferson, he entered into questionable relations with England which helped to persuade that nation not to push matters with the United States and to let events take their course. He aided in producing a belief in England that, in case of war, New England would abandon the United States, and he assisted materially in the erection of a British party in America that seemed to be the living proof of the representations he had made to George H. Rose. At the head of this party he forced the surrender of the Embargo and restored New England to the guidance of Federalism.

TIMOTHY PICKERING AND THE WAR
OF 1812.

By Hervey Putnam Prentiss.

When the Twelfth Congress assembled in the fall of 1811, the event which Timothy Pickering had been predicting for years seemed to be at hand. This Congress, controlled by a vigorous group of young "War-Hawks," was not disposed to follow the pacific and temporizing policies of Jefferson and Madison. Driven by an ardent nationalism and an insatiable desire for territorial expansion, these men were impatient of the restraints imposed on American commerce by the European belligerents and were loud in their advocacy of war. Consequently, Congress entered at once into a discussion of American foreign relations and a consideration of measures that could have only one meaning—war with England. That these men from the interior should feel so much concern for the rights of merchants and sailors in a time when sectional interests were the most powerful motives of political action may seem at first glance surprising, but the secret of their ardor may be found in certain of their public utterances, which inseparably connected territorial expansion with a war for national rights.[1]

The combination of an English war and territorial expansion could not fail to be hateful to the Federalists. If the western Republicans had consciously selected issues designed to irritate their opponents, they could not have done it better than with these two projects. Yet most Federalist Congressmen voted for the preparedness measures undertaken by the "War-Hawks" in the session of

[1] See Julius Pratt, *Expansionists of 1812* (New York, 1925), for a scholarly exposition of the expansionist activities of the "War-Hawks."

1811-12, although they did not lend their aid to the demand for war with England. Their purposes were scarcely those of patriotically supporting the government in preparing to protest vigorously against the violation of American rights. Instead, it was their hope that the war would be mismanaged and would discredit the administration, thus giving them the chance to rise to power on the ruins of the Republican party.[2] By supporting the war measures, the Federalists would free themselves from the charge that they had hampered the administration in its conduct of the war and had thus brought defeat upon the nation.[3] So certain of the wisdom of this strategy were some of the Federalists that two of them approached the British minister, Augustus J. Foster, with the suggestion that he advise his government not to revoke or modify the Orders in Council. Such a concession, they said, would seem to justify the restrictive system and lead to its indefinite continuance, while a firm stand on the part of the British would lead to a war which must result in the ruin of the Republican administration and the victory of the Federalist party. Then, as the Federalists told Foster, it would be easy to reach an agreement by which their party and Great Britain would both be the gainers.[4]

To this program of supporting a war in the hope of discrediting the ruling party, Timothy Pickering was unalterably opposed. Although he had lost his seat in the Senate as a result of Republican victories in Massachusetts in 1810 and 1811,[5] he was a man of great prestige

[2] Morison, *Otis*, II, 34-35.

[3] Pickering MSS. (Massachusetts Historical Society), William Reed to Pickering, Jan. 20, 1812.

[4] Correspondence of Augustus J. Foster, Jan.-Mar., 1812, Public Record Office, London, F. O. 5, Vol. 84 (Library of Congress Photostats), Foster to Wellesley, Feb. 2, 1812.

[5] After the state election of 1810, the Republicans attempted to unseat Pickering, but failed to do so as the Federalists still controlled half of the upper house of the Massachusetts legislature. As a result, Pickering's continuance in office became a major issue in the campaign of 1811. Thereupon, the Senator entered directly into the contest with a public appeal in the form of a series of letters, *Mr. Pickering's Address to the People of the United States*, printed in many Federalist newspapers and later published as a pamphlet. These letters, which at-

in the party. In fact, he seemed to consider himself a party leader who should, from his Wenham farm, direct the policies of Federalist Congressmen and Senators. His whole political philosophy was outraged by this seeming support of war with England. To Senator Dana of Connecticut he expressed his views in no uncertain terms as he advised him that Federalists should cease to vote for the war resolutions and the measures associated with them. He saw "no force" in the argument that it had always been a Federalist policy to supply the nation with adequate means of defence.

"By such concurrence," he wrote, "perhaps federal gentlemen imagine they shall expose to derision and unpopularity (if I may use the word) Porter & his whole bullying gang of warriors, who, these gentlemen believe, have no intention to go to war with G. Britain. But those bullies bid defiance to shame—as valorously as they appear to defy the power of Britain. They, like their leaders, Jefferson & Madison, are so destitute of dignity, of the honourable feelings, as to disregard the just reproaches of the most intelligent, & respectable citizens, & to prefer to *their* approbation the empty applause of the uninformed & deluded populace, whose suffrages are necessary to the maintenance of their power. That Jefferson . . . & his followers, blind, ignorant, or unprincipled, do not intend active war with Great Britain I perfectly believe: but that a war of *mere endurance* on our part, in which they would take care to make G. Britain appear the aggressor, a war that should only destroy our commerce would be unwelcome to Jefferson I am far from thinking. For with all the clamors of his ignorant & corrupt partisans, of British injustice, violence, & outrage, he does not think they would burn a single town or city on our sea coast. But such a passive war would save him and his party a world of trouble in contriving miserable and disgraceful shifts to soothe their Lord Napoleon and to impoverish the commercial states &

tempted to vindicate their author's course and attack the Republican policies, were mainly repetitions of arguments long familiar to Pickering's followers. Although highly regarded by regular Federalists, the letters won no new converts for the party, and Federalism was decisively defeated in a bitter campaign. Consequently, the Republican legislature proceeded in June, 1811, to elect Joseph Varnum to succeed Timothy Pickering in the Senate of the United States.

Jefferson will be content to see our great places of foreign trade gradually decay; or if burnt by the British in such a war, he calculates on an exaggerated hostility to that nation —not on the curses of the people against the real authors of their destruction." [6]

Thus, from the very beginning, Pickering set himself resolutely against a war with England. It was his opinion that Federalists should oppose every war measure and refuse their support in such a war. The only results of war which he could see were the destruction of the commercial interests and some aid to Napoleon in his fight with England. In fact, he believed that these were the real purposes of the war party and that even the conquest of Canada was a cloak for them. If Canada should be conquered, he was sure that it would be turned over to Napoleon, who desired it as one step in reviving the French empire in America.[7] Yet, in spite of this gloomy outlook, he saw one ray of hope that war might serve to bring the people of New England to their senses and restore them to the fold of Federalism. If Great Britain should conduct the war in a "magnanimous spirit," as he was sure it would, he believed that the contrast between the policies of Britain and those of the Jeffersonians would soon be seen, and then another Federalist revival, like that of 1808-09, would surely take place in the northern states.[8] In a few weeks his hope seemed to have some justification, for the mere threat of war was beginning to bring Massachusetts back to Federalism.

The possibility of war was an opportunity for the Massachusetts Federalists. Once again could the election call go forth that the policy of the administration endangered the commercial interests of the northern states. Early in February the state party organization issued "An Address to the Free and Independent People of Massachusetts," declaring that the object of the administration was to "keep alive the existing irritations against Britain, and to break down the commercial strength of Massachusetts, by continued restrictions," and calling on

[6] Pickering MSS., Pickering to Dana, Jan. 16, 1812.
[7] *Ibid.*, Pickering to William Reed, Jan. 30, 1812.
[8] *Ibid.*, Pickering to Dana, Feb. 17, 1812.

the voters to elect Caleb Strong governor as the first step in defeating the designs of men hostile to commerce.[9] National issues were once more to be prominent in a state election as the Federalists took advantage of the growing resentment of the people against the coming war. In addition, local political conditions were favorable to the Federalist cause, for the administration of Governor Gerry had not won great popularity. He had filled most of the state offices with his own followers; he had instituted many libel suits against the Federalist press; and he had redistricted the state in the manner since known as "gerrymandering," with a view to retaining Republican predominance in the State Senate. These actions had laid him open to charges of unconstitutional behavior which were made frequently during the campaign.[10]

This combination of local unpopularity and an important national issue was in a fair way to produce a Federalist reaction when the disclosure of the "Henry Plot" was made by President Madison. While the information sold by John Henry for fifty thousand dollars actually proved little, Republicans hoped it would discredit their opponents by branding them with the stigma of having engaged in a treasonable plot to bring about the secession of New England with British aid.[11] But the Henry letters were less significant than the majority party wished them to be. Although the administration made every attempt to get them before the people,[12] the Federalists had more success in pointing to them as a "cheap, elec-

9 Salem Gazette, Feb. 11, 1812.

10 Barry, History of Massachusetts, III, 367-69.

11 Foster's Correspondence, Foster to Wellesley, Mar. 9, 10, 12, 1812. Foster predicted that the Henry letters would lead to a Republican victory in Massachusetts and reported that "The Federalists complain severely of us and say that whenever they are on the eve of carrying their wishes into effect of producing a cordial reconciliation between the two Countries something happens on the part of the British to prostrate their efforts."

12 As an example of Republican propaganda, see The Essex Junto and the British Spry; or, Treason Detected, a pamphlet published at Salem in March, 1812, which printed the Henry letters with an introduction designed to prove that a "Junto" conspiracy of several years standing was working for the dissolution of the Union.

tioneering trick."[13]   The Boston Federalists, who were especially implicated by Henry's charges, utterly denied any connection with the plot and publicly declared that they were devoted to the Union.   Their resolutions endeavored to make it clear that while they clung to the Union as their "best hope," they did not forget that *"to preserve and protect Commerce were the principle motives of the People of this Commonwealth in acceding to it,"* a declaration especially calculated to appeal to the dominant commercial classes in the election.[14]

Less than two weeks after the Henry disclosures, the Massachusetts electorate heard of another "plot."   One Timothy Medey Joy of Middleton, New Hampshire, apparently inspired by election talk and by the notoriety won by John Henry, appeared in Haverhill, Massachusetts, under the name of Nathaniel Emery.   Claiming that he had been an officer in the British army, he told a group of citizens that he knew of certain treasonable correspondence between Timothy Pickering and Colonel James Hamilton, a British officer in Canada.[15]   Haverhill Republicans, believing that they had made a discovery of importance, persuaded Joy to sign an affidavit to the effect that he had certain knowledge of this correspondence.   Joy then went on to Salem, where he told the same story, but at the same time Federalist leaders of Haverhill sent word to Salem that they believed Joy to be an imposter.[16]   There he was arrested, taken before a justice of the peace, and forced to admit that his story was false and that Emery was an assumed name.[17]   Having succeeded in proving Joy an imposter, the Federalists now proceeded to capitalize on their opponents' haste to accept an unauthenticated story for the purposes of the election.   It was now their turn to make charges of a plot.   In an election handbill, they alleged that a group of "Jacobin demagogues" in Haverhill were responsible

[13] *Columbian Centinel*, Mar. 21, 1812; Pickering MSS., William Reed to Pickering, Mar. 11, 1812.
[14] *Salem Gazette*, Mar. 31, 1812.
[15] Pickering MSS., Copy of certificate of Timothy Medey Joy, Mar. 20, 1812.
[16] *Ibid.*, John Varnum to Samuel Putnam, Mar. 20, 1812.
[17] *Salem Gazette*, Mar. 24, 1812.

for introducing Pickering's name into Joy's story and
that in this they were inspired only by political motives.[18]
The Republicans responded, in another handbill, that Joy
himself had first mentioned Pickering's name and that
the Republicans of Haverhill, who had heard him, had
acted only as honest men, anxious to suppress treason.[19]
But the harm had been done and nothing could effectively counteract the impression that the Republicans had
trumped up false charges against Pickering. As a result,
the former Senator's popularity was enhanced, and a few
days later at a Federalist gathering in Boston, he was
received with great applause.[20]

On election day, the Federalists reaped the fruits of
Republican errors and of the unpopular war measures of
Congress, as they carried the state by 52,696 to 51,326.[21]
But the State Senate, thanks to Gerry's skill in redistricting, remained Republican by twenty-nine to eleven,[22]
although it was clear that of the whole number of votes
cast in the election of Senators the majority was Federalist.[23] "Thus we see," said the *Salem Gazette,* "that by
cutting and carving and *packing* Districts, a *minority* of
voters elect nearly three-fourths of the Senate."[24]

Encouraged by the showing of his party, Pickering
once more entered the lists with a series of "Letters to
the People of Massachusetts," designed this time to secure
the election of a Federalist majority to the lower house
of the Legislature.[25] His appeal was the old one, a call

[18] *Another Plot, the heat of Election hatches a Brood of Plots
and Falsehoods.*
[19] *Beware of Imposters, or Slander Detected.*
[20] Bentley, *Diary,* IV, 91.
[21] *Salem Gazette,* June 2, 1812.
[22] *Ibid.,* May 18, 1812.
[23] *Columbian Centinel,* May 20, 1812. The total of the Federalist vote for the Senate was 51,766, while the Republican total
was 50,164.
[24] May 18, 1812.
[25] *Salem Gazette,* May 5, 8, 15, 1812. The *Register* (May 5,
1812) commented, "The Lie-on of Federalism has (to the great
neglect of his little farm) entered again into the political *world
seeking whom he may devour,*" and the *Boston Patriot* (May 9,
1812) remarked, "This old veteran in political iniquity has commenced another series of letters on public affairs, addressed to
the people of Massachusetts; intended to promote the holy
cause of federalism in the pending election for representatives
in that State."

to the people of the state to defend the commercial interests from the attacks of Jefferson and Madison, which
he again declared to be dictated by France.   The old
story of the Embargo brought about by French influence
was brushed up and republished.   The new Embargo, supposed to be a measure preparatory to war was denounced
in the same terms and attributed to the same influence.
As before, Pickering predicted that the administration
would soon lead the nation into a war with England.
For this war he could see but one cause, the influence
of Napoleon, who could not possibly defeat England without some aid from the United States.   Taking up the
Florida question, he asserted, as he had done in the Senate more than a year earlier,[26] that the United States had
no claim to that region, and that that was known to be
the case when the Louisiana Treaty was signed in 1803.
American aggression in Florida, he pointed out, was likely
to lead to war, as England would resent unjustifiable
encroachments on the territory of her ally, Spain.   If
war should come, he predicted dire consequences, for it
would surely involve the destruction of the commercial
life of Massachusetts, which would, in turn, lead straight
to the dissolution of the Union.   The remedy, he told
the people, lay in the hands of the citizens of Massachusetts, who, by returning a Federalist House of Representatives, could serve a warning on the national government before it was too late.

The number of Massachusetts voters who agreed with this
view was apparently increasing, for the Federalists were
eminently successful in the election, securing 423 Representatives to 294 for the Republicans.[27]   In Salem, where
the party of Jefferson had maintained a precarious majority for some years, the Federalists or "Washingtonians"
elected all thirteen of their candidates, while the "Em-
bargoroons" as the *Gazette* styled them, failed to elect
a single man.   Among those chosen were John Pickering,
Jr., and Samuel Putnam, and thus the victory of the party
became a sort of personal triumph for the Pickering
family.[28]

[26] *Annals of Congress*, 11th, 3rd, 65-66.
[27] *Salem Gazette*, May 18, 1812.
[28] *Ibid.*, May 15, 1812.

If the April and May elections had any significance
beyond a merely local reaction to the policies of Elbridge
Gerry and his Republican supporters, they meant that the
voters of Massachusetts had delivered an opinion adverse
to the war measures of Congress. If Pickering's appeal
had any meaning, it is reasonable to interpret the Federalist victory as a mandate to the Legislature to adopt
measures warning the national government that Massachusetts disapproved its course and would offer a vigorous opposition to the war with England. At any rate,
the House of Representatives accepted the election as
proof that the people of Massachusetts did not wish war.
On the motion of Samuel Putnam, the House voted, on
June 3, to petition Congress "to avert the evil of impending war." [29] Pickering's policy of complete opposition to
the war was quite evidently preferred to the strategy of
pushing matters toward a war that might discredit the
Madison administration. Within the ranks of the party
there was little dissent, for the petition was railroaded
through without debate and passed by a strictly party
vote of 402 to 278. [30]

Next, the House turned to consider the Governor's message, which, as usual, dwelt much on national affairs.
In its answer, the House once more declared its opposition to an English war. Deploring the "mysterious ties"
which seemed to bind the nation to France, it expressed
the hope that the United States would "never engage in
any but a just and necessary war." In its opinion, war
with Great Britain would not fall within that category,
for it declared that there was no point at issue which could
not be adjusted by a sincere attempt at negotiation. Such
a war must be ruinous to the commercial states, said the
House, as it warned the national government that it would
not be deterred from expressing its opinions freely on the
expediency of hostilities with England and that during the
war it would not hesitate to discuss the measures and conduct of the administration. [31] In effect, the General Court
was warning the government that Massachusetts would fol-

[29] *Salem Gazette*, June 5, 1812.
[30] *Ibid.*, June 5, 1812.
[31] *Ibid.*, June 16, 1812.

low the course it had taken in 1809, if Congress persisted in going contrary to the desires of the commercial interests.[32] Two centers of Federalism, Boston, which had never departed from the leadership of that party, and Salem, now controlled by the Pickering group, hastened to assure the lower house of the correctness of its attitude, as they adopted resolutions echoing and praising the opinions of the "Address to Congress" and the "Answer to Governor Strong." [33] Once more town meetings became active and if the declaration of war had not intervened at this point, the government would in all likelihood have been immediately assailed by numerous petitions and resolutions as it had been in 1808-09.

In the meantime the Republicans were not silent. The minority of the Massachusetts House of Representatives entered its protest against the "Address to Congress." Believing that its adoption was intended merely to embarrass the administration and that a single branch of the Legislature had no right to interfere in matters belonging exclusively to Congress, it assured the Congressional leaders of its support in a war with England.[34] Nor was the Republican press inclined to take the action of the Federalists without a vigorous protest.

"We were in hopes," said the *Boston Patriot,* "that the Federalists would by this time have learnt wisdom; but *Faction* is again rearing its head, and an opposition is showing itself once more against the national government. The people are to be once more alarmed and excited by a false representation that Congress is going to plunge the country into ruin. That *Faction* deserves the execration of every honest American who wickedly strives to sow discord between the State and General Government. . . . The *American nation* is about declaring open, fair, and honorable war against one of the most insidious enemies that ever encumbered the earth since the days of Carthage. . . ." [35]

[32] The Republicans charged that this was the purpose of the Federalists. See "Federalism of 1809—revived.." in the *Boston Patriot,* June 6, 1812.
[33] *Columbian Centinel,* June 13, 17, 1812; *Salem Gazette,* June 23, 1812.
[34] *Boston Patriot,* June 13, 1812.
[35] *Ibid.,* June 6, 1812.

Before the Federalist protests could be of any avail, Congress declared war against Great Britain, and the opposition to an "impending war" merged into more violent declarations against an existing war. In Salem a town meeting was called for June 24, to replace its address to Congress by a petition to the Legislature asking that steps be taken immediately for the relief of the state. Other towns prepared to take similar action and plans were made to call county conventions to protest against the war.[36] The House of Representatives received these appeals with approval and declared that it was natural for the towns to look to the Legislature for relief. Repeating its earlier assertion that there was no real cause for war with England, it announced that the so-called causes for war were only pretexts. The actual causes of the war, it said, were the willingness of the government to serve Bonaparte and the desire "to aggrandize the Southern and Western States at the expense of the Eastern section of the Union." As a practical measure, it recommended:

"Organize a *peace party* throughout your country, and let all other party distinctions vanish, . . . meet and consult together for the common good in your towns and counties. . . . Express your sentiments without fear, and let the sound of your disapprobation of this war be loud and deep. Let it be distinctly understood, that in support of it your conformity to the requisitions of law will be the result of principle and not of choice. If your sons must be torn from you by conscription, consign them to the care of GOD; but let there be no volunteers except for defensive war." [37]

The response was general and immediate. From all quarters came declarations, memorials, and resolutions. The Ipswich town meeting on June 25 condemned the war as due to subserviency to France, hostility to the commercial interests of New England, and prejudice against the English. Avowing its willingness to use all lawful means to "effect a change of rulers," it expressed a desire to co-operate with other towns to secure peace

[36] *Salem Gazette*, June 26, 1812.
[37] *Address of the House of Representatives to the People of Massachusetts* (Boston, 1812).

through the organization of committees of correspondence to work for that end.[38]   On June 29, Newbury and Newburyport adopted resolutions of similar import.   In addition, Newburyport suggested that the state should recognize only the Governor as commander of the state militia and refuse to permit the state troops to serve under the federal government.[39]   On June 30, Gloucester boldly announced:

"To our State Government we look for firm, dignified, and prompt measures, such as will do honor to the sons of freemen—such as will break in pieces the chains prepared to bind us to the car of the Corsican—that destroyer of liberty and nations—and if our blood must flow, let it issue from a thousand wounds, to preserve those who may survive the struggle from slavery and all its attendant horrors." [40]

On July 15, the Boston town meeting condemned the war and declared that it would oppose it by all means short of forcible resistance.[41]   On August 6, another set of resolutions issued from Boston to suggest that a state convention be held to perfect measures against the war.[42] Although the suggestion was seriously considered by Federalists, it did not bear fruit.   From the interior as well as from the sea coast came protests against the war, until it seemed as if all parts of the state were being knit together to hamper the prosecution of the war.[43]

Following the protests of the towns, county conventions were called to draw up resolutions of opposition.   Essex County, under Pickering's lead, was in the field early, but the first step was taken by the three Connecticut River counties.   Although twenty-five years earlier "Old Hampshire" had been the scene of the activities of Daniel Shays, it was in 1812 the strongest center of conservative Federalism in the state.   On July 14, the representatives of fifty-three legal town meetings and of Federalist gath-

[38] *Salem Gazette*, July 3, 1812.
[39] *Ibid.*, July 7, 1812.
[40] *Ibid.*, July 10, 1812.
[41] *Columbian Centinel*, July 18, 1812.
[42] *Ibid.*, Aug. 8, 1812.
[43] Resolutions from such inland towns as Springfield, Northampton, and Gorham, may be seen in the columns of the *Gazette* and the *Centinel* during July and August.

erings in three additional towns met at Northampton to
adopt a memorial to the President and twenty anti-war
resolutions which threatened everything but "forcible resistance" and disunion.[44] On July 21, the Essex County
convention sat at Ipswich, with Timothy Pickering in
the chair. Its resolutions incorporated most of Pickering's
ideas on the war and were commonly believed to have been
written by him. Anticipating the Boston resolutions of
August 6, the Essex meeting called for a convention of
county delegates to meet at Boston to determine "the
surest means of restoring peace and commerce." [45] Before
two weeks more had passed, Essex and "Old Hampshire"
were joined by Barnstable, Bristol, Lincoln, Middlesex,
Plymouth, and Worcester counties in their declarations
against the war.[46]

Knowing full well the hatred of the orthodox clergy for
Jefferson and his policies, the Federalist leaders made a
successful bid for the support of the ministry in whipping
up the anti-war spirit, as Governor Strong proclaimed
July 23 a day of fast, humiliation, and prayer, because

"it has pleased the Almighty Ruler of the world in his right-
eous Providence to permit us to engage in a war against the
nation from whom we are descended, and which for many
years has been the bulwark of the Religion we profess." [47]

Though it was many a month before Republicans would
allow Caleb Strong to forget these words, there were few
clergymen who did not agree with their sentiments and
who were not willing to proclaim the principles of Federalism from their pulpits, as did the Reverend David Osgood of Medford when he preached his Fast Day sermon
on the text, "Fight ye not against the Lord God of your
fathers; for ye shall not prosper."[48]

While the tone of the Federalist protest was so strong
that the Republicans alleged that their opponents aimed

[44] *Columbian Centinel*, July 25, 1812.
[45] Pickering, *Declaration of the County of Essex, Convention
at Ipswich, 21 July 1812.*
[46] *Columbian Centinel*, July and August, 1812.
[47] *Salem Gazette*, June 30, 1812.
[48] Rev. David Osgood, *A solemn protest against the late declaration of war; discourse, 1812.*

at the dissolution of the Union,[49] it cannot be said that
secession was seriously proposed as a remedy in 1812.
Since the Henry disclosures, men were more cautious in
making statements that might be interpreted as evidence
of a disunion plot.   Practically all resolutions and appeals
were careful to include pledges of allegiance to the Union
and to advocate only such measures as fell short of "forcible resistance."   It is true that some Federalist editors
indulged themselves in such remarks as, "We suppose no
person of observation had believed that the Union, in its
present extent, could last for ages,"[50] and "The Union is
dear . . . But Commerce is still more dear," [51] but these
expressions of opinion can scarcely be considered evidence
of any widespread disunion sentiment.   The utmost that
Federalist leaders were willing to recommend in the summer of 1812 were open refusal to support the war and
passive resistance to the measures of the government.   The
truth is that they were looking to the presidential election
with renewed hope in the expectation that the unpopularity
of the war might at least result in the choice of a northern
Republican who would be friendly to commerce.   The
resolution of the Ipswich town meeting, "to use all lawful
means to effect a change of rulers," [52] lay close to the
center of Federalist activity in 1812.

In the Federalist revival and the proceedings against
the war, the influence of Timothy Pickering has been noted
at certain points and one is led to ask how far the character of the anti-war movement was in accord with his
ideas.   Obviously his publications helped to determine the
issue of the spring elections and were extremely influential
in forming the program of opposition.   His only private
letter of importance at this time indicates that the measures taken in Massachusetts were in almost exact agreement with his opinions.   On July 6, Edward Pennington,
a Philadelphia Federalist, wrote to ask for confidential
advice and to inquire whether men could expect the Union

---

49 *Salem Register*, Aug. 5, 1812.
50 *Salem Gazette*, July 2, 1812.
51 *Columbian Centinel*, July 25, 1812.
52 *Salem Gazette*, July 3, 1812.

to last much longer.[53] Pickering answered that he would
preserve the Union if possible, but added, "There is no
magic in my ears in the sound of Union." If it should
be impossible to maintain the objects of the Union as he
conceived them, he favored its destruction. Yet he felt
that the South and West would be unwilling to allow the
northern states to go their own way, as both were closely
bound to the North by economic considerations. If the separation of New England were threatened, he believed that
the South and West would yield to Northern demands
rather than allow secession to take place. But, in his
opinion, it was unnecessary to go that far. The war, much
as he deplored it, seemed necessary, he said, "to convince
the people that their rulers must be changed." He added
that he was confident of that result in all of New England
and New York. Apparently he felt that the Federalists
could not win without effort, for he told Pennington that
he was "for bold and decisive measures, but ones perfectly
compatible with the Constitution and the Union of the
States," lest "the unprincipled men" who had "betrayed"
the nation should be encouraged to continue.[54] The whole
tenor of this advice was in perfect harmony with the measures that had been taken in Massachusetts.

In speaking of "bold and decisive measures" that were
"perfectly compatible with the Constitution," Pickering
was, of course, speaking of the Constitution in terms of
strict construction, for Massachusetts and her sister states
of New England were even then preparing to refuse the
use of their militia forces to the national government and
defending their action on constitutional grounds. Obviously, such refusal could be based only on a complete
denial of the doctrine of implied powers. Although the
Constitution declared that "Congress may provide for calling forth the militia to execute the laws of the Union, suppress insurrection, and repel invasion," the Massachusetts
Supreme Court practically denied the right of the national
government to control the militia in any way, as it asserted:

[53] Pickering MSS., Pennington to Pickering, July 6, 1812.
[54] Adams, *New England Federalism*, 388-90, Pickering to Pennington, July 12, 1812.

". . . no power is given, either to the President or Congress, to determine that either of the said exigencies do in fact exist . . . and from the nature of the power, it must be exercised by those with whom the states have respectively entrusted the chief command of the militia." [55]

Connecticut, too, adopted a similar opinion, as its General Assembly stated emphatically:

"But it must not be forgotten, that the state of Connecticut is a FREE SOVEREIGN and INDEPENDENT state; that the United States are a *confederacy* of states; that we are a confederated and not a consolidated republic." [56]

If the high Federalists had any doubt as to the popularity of this type of program in New England, the fall elections must surely have dispelled it. Not since the administration of John Adams had they won such a sweeping victory. New England and New York went solidly for the "peace ticket" and DeWitt Clinton, and Federalist strength in the House of Representatives was doubled.[57] Among the new Federalist Congressmen was Timothy Pickering. On the day after the election, the *Salem Gazette* announced triumphantly:

"In Essex North District, that venerable and long-tried Patriot, the Hon. Timothy Pickering, is elected by a vast majority of votes; so that the whole of Essex, notwithstanding all the cuttings and carvings of our political *butchers,* will be represented by men of the old Washington School." [58]

But overwhelming victories in the northern states could not elect a President, nor could they force the adminis-

55 Ames, *State Documents*, II, 14.
56 *Ibid.*, 17.
57 Adams, *History of the United States*, VI, 413.
58 Nov. 3, 1812. The redistricting of Massachusetts had placed Pickering's town of Wenham in the Essex North District. It was practically conceded in advance to the Federalists, as the Republicans refused even to nominate a candidate to oppose Pickering. The South District was expected to remain Republican, as it included the strongest centers of Republicanism. However, the Federalist revival was so great that even there a Federalist, William Read, was chosen by the decisive vote of 2,403 to 1,877. Republicans were inclined to explain part of their loss of votes on the ground that many men who would normally have voted for their candidates were then away from home on privateering expeditions.

tration to abandon the war. As a consequence, the Federalist opposition became increasingly radical and it was not long before the party press began to offer suggestions of disunion. "By continuing this ruinous War and placing us between the upper and nether millstones, the War party manifestly intend to drive us forcibly from the union," wrote the editor of the *Salem Gazette*.[59] A few weeks later, "Massachusetts" in the *Columbian Centinel* was voicing the now familiar complaint that the addition of new states to the Union was depriving the older states of their just influence and gradually forcing the Northeast out of the Union.[60] Always the tendency was to describe themselves as being driven from the Union, never to advocate positive steps toward secession.

The opinions of the editors were close to Pickering's. Since the Federalists had failed to elect their presidential candidate or to secure a majority in Congress, it was clear that they could not hope to end the war or change the policy of the administration by the ordinary modes of political action. Their only hope lay in the concerted action of the states opposed to the war or in the threat of secession. They saw that their efforts to hamper the conduct of the war by refusing militia service had met with success. Even Madison admitted that.[61] Naturally this success suggested that other measures of a similar nature might put the Federalist minority in a position to accomplish its purposes.

To such a course of radical opposition Pickering was definitely committed. After the fall election, he had suggested that New England take further steps to halt the progress of the war, but Chief Justice Parsons had attempted to satisfy him by saying that the Massachusetts Legislature would act during its winter session.[62] How-

59 Dec. 4, 1812.
60 Dec., 1812, and Jan., 1813.
61 Madison, *Writings* (Gaillard Hunt, ed., 9 vols., New York, 1900), VIII, 210-14, Madison to Jefferson, Aug. 17, 1812, "The seditious opposition in Massachusetts and Connecticut with intrigues elsewhere insidiously co-operating with it has so clogged the wheels of war that I fear the campaign will not accomplish its object."
62 Adams, *New England Federalism*, 404-06, Pickering to John Lowell, Nov. 7, 1814.

ever, the Legislature, under the control of moderate Federalists, was not ready for an immediate and vigorous opposition to the national administration. The measures which it adopted were so weak as to be almost frivolous in nature. One was the creation of a special committee to ascertain the number of Massachusetts seamen who had been impressed by the British. The motion had come from John Pickering, Jr., and was probably suggested by his father.[63] Its purpose was to prove that British impressments were insignificant in number and that the administration was using the impressment issue as a cloak to cover the real cause of war. The report of the committee, of which John Pickering, Jr., was chairman, declared, as one would expect, that the number of impressed Massachusetts seamen was but slightly more than one hundred, and that the total from the entire nation could not possibly exceed a few hundred. The investigations and final report of the committee received due publicity in the Federalist press and were used to keep the anti-war spirit at its height in New England.[64]

The nature of the Massachusetts opposition was well illustrated by another measure passed at this session. It had been proposed that the state build a 74-gun ship of the line and offer it to the federal government for the duration of the war, but the committee to whom this proposal had been referred, reported that it deemed such action inexpedient. Adopting the report of the committee, the Legislature declared:

"It is the right and duty of the citizens to examine the conduct of their rulers, by all lawful means to oppose such measures as appear to them impolitic or unjust. Instead, therefore, of contributing their voluntary aid to the present ruinous and destructive war, it is to be expected and most ardently hoped that the state of Massachusetts will continue with increasing unanimity, in every constitutional mode to oppose that system of measures which has so long oppressed this portion of the country; and to restore to the commercial

63 *Niles' Register*, Feb. 20, 1813.
64 *Salem Gazette, Columbian Centinel*, various dates in 1813. The substance of the report was given by Pickering in the House of Representatives in his speech on the loan bill, Feb. 26, 28, 1814. (*Annals of Congress*, 13th, 2nd, 1697-1750.)

states that influence in the councils of the union, to which
by their population, their wealth, and their physical strength,
they are so justly entitled." [65]

Irritating as such action might be to the administration
supporters, it could scarcely be expected to accomplish
anything when accompanied by no more positive measures.

The hesitation of the Massachusetts Federalists to follow Pickering's lead was due to their desire to await the
results of the spring election. Fearing to proceed on the
basis of existing majorities only, they hoped to strengthen
their hold on New England and to carry New York, whose
aid seemed absolutely essential to the success of any anti-
administration movement in the North. Disappointed at
this turn of events, Pickering again appealed directly to
the people. In March he began a series of public letters
designed to serve the interests of the party in the approaching election and direct the course of the New England
opposition.[66]

The letters were written in Pickering's usual style,
wordy and discursive, but they did not mince words on
the question of supporting the government in war. Believing the war "unnecessary, unjust, wanton, and profli-
gate," the author declared that he could not vote men and
money for it. He was still of the opinion that Jefferson
and Madison did not want a treaty of amity with England, for they had made the abandonment of impressment
a *sine qua non,* when that was an impossible condition for
Great Britain to accept.[67] But his heaviest fire was reserved for the financial policy of the administration, as he
attacked the war loans. He told his readers that there
was nothing in the history of Republican financial policy
to warrant a belief that the government would be able to
repay these loans. The Republicans, he said, had repudiated the sound principles of Hamilton's financial system,
designed to establish the national credit; they had proclaimed economy in government while they were hypo-
critically increasing the nation's debt; and, rejecting inter-

[65] *Niles' Register,* Mar. 20, 1813.
[66] *Salem Gazette,* Mar. 12-Apr. 20, 1813, "Letters to the People
of the United States."
[67] *Ibid.,* Mar. 12, 1813.

nal taxes, they had sought to place the burden of public
finance on commerce, even while they were destroying
that commerce by Embargo and Non-Intercourse.[68] As
for the existing financial situation, he predicted that Congress would not vote taxes sufficient to guarantee the re-
payment of the war debt. The burden of voting such
taxes, he said, must rest on the war party, as Federalists
and peace Republicans would oppose them on principle,
while the southerners and westerners supporting the war
would not dare risk unpopularity by imposing heavy
taxes.[69]

"For myself," he declared, "as a member of the National
Legislature, having deliberately considered the subject, I
explicitly declare, that I do not hold myself under any obli-
gation to give my vote to redeem the paper money called
exchequer bills, issued and issuing by the secretary of the
treasury, or the loans of millions on millions which he is
now attempting to effect, to continue this unnecessary and
iniquitous war." [70]

In New England the results of the spring elections were
highly gratifying to the Federalists. New Hampshire,
which had hitherto upheld the war, went Federalist as
John Taylor Gilman defeated William Plumer by a close
vote.[71] In Massachusetts Caleb Strong was re-elected by
a far larger majority than he had won in 1812.[72] In the
Legislature, the Massachusetts Federalists were equally
successful, as they secured control of the Senate by twenty-
six to nine and of the House of Representatives by 403
to 159.[73] Even the "Gerrymander" senatorial district of
Essex County was carried by the Federalists.[74] But their
hope of winning New York was blasted as Governor Tomp-
kins defeated Stephen Van Rensselaer. Yet there was a
grain of comfort in securing a small majority in the New
York Assembly.[75]

[68] *Salem Gazette*, Mar. 19, 1813.
[69] *Ibid.*, Mar. 16, 1813.
[70] *Ibid.*, Mar. 5, 1813.
[71] *Ibid.*, Mar. 5, 1813.
[72] *Ibid.*, June 1, 1813; Strong, 56,754; Varnum, 42,789.
[73] *Ibid.*, May 28, 1813.
[74] *Ibid.*, Apr. 6, 1813.
[75] Adams, *History of the United States*, VII, 49-50.

Encouraged by these gains, Massachusetts proceeded to opposition measures of some consequence, though less extreme than Pickering desired. Before the new Legislature met, the keynote was struck by Josiah Quincy in an address to the Washington Benevolent Society of Boston. In this address he revived the old issues of western expansion and the admission of new states, as he pointed to them as fundamental causes for the distress of New England. Slave representation, too, came in for severe criticism at his hands. Attributing the war and the ruin of commerce to southern and western influence, he called on the commercial states to unite in support of constitutional measures to alter the system which oppressed them.[76]

Quincy's suggestion met with the full approval of the Federalist radicals. Pickering was so pleased that he asked for several copies of the speech to distribute among his friends.[77] Gouverneur Morris, whose opinions were even more extreme, regarded the reformation of the Constitution as more essential to the northern states than the withholding of war supplies.[78] Being thus assured of the support of the radicals, Quincy undertook the task of leading the Massachusetts Legislature to adopt a program of protest which included proposals to prohibit the admission of new states from areas outside the original territory of the United States, and to declare the admission of Louisiana unconstitutional.

In response to Quincy's leadership and the "Speech" of Governor Strong, which officially called attention to this question as well as to other problems arising out of the relation of Massachusetts to the federal government,[79] both houses of the Legislature united in the adoption of a series of resolutions declaring unconstitutional the admission of states from areas outside the original limits of the nation, and demanding the repeal of the act of April 8, 1812, which had admitted Louisiana to the

76 Edmund Quincy, *Life of Josiah Quincy* (Boston, 1874), 310-16.

77 *Ibid.*, 318-19.

78 *Ibid.*, 317-18; Jared Sparks, *Life of Gouverneur Morris with selections from his correspondence and miscellaneous papers* (3 vols., Boston, 1832), III, 292-93.

79 *Niles' Register*, June 12, 1813.

Union. The increasingly hostile temper of Massachusetts was evident in the second resolution, which asserted:

". . . it is the interest and duty of the people of Massachusetts, to oppose the admission of such States into the Union, as a measure tending to the dissolution of the confederacy." [80]

Nor was this all. The Governor had urged the adoption of general remonstrances against the war and had called for further support of his stand on the militia question. In retaliation for his refusal to muster the militia for the service of the national government, the War Department had refused to supply the state with its quota of arms.[81]   Both houses now hastened to assure Strong of the correctness of the position he had taken.   Asserting that "their right and duty of free inquiry into the grounds and origins" of the war would not be surrendered without a struggle, they announced that they were not bound to support an unjust war and that the action of the War Department was unconstitutional.[82] After this declaration of principles, the Legislature instructed the State Treasurer to withhold from the national government a part of the state tax equal to the value of the arms that should have been given to the state.[83] This measure was supplemented by a formal "Remonstrance" which summarized all the war-time grievances against the administration. The document was addressed to Congress and sent to Pickering to present to the House of Representatives.[84]

As an instance of the lengths to which Massachusetts' opposition to the war was carried, the action of the Legislature in regard to Captain Lawrence is illuminating. As commander of the *Hornet* at the time of its victory over the *Peacock* in the spring of 1813, he had become a national hero, but Massachusetts refused to join in the general praise which was bestowed on him. When it was

[80] Ames, *State Documents*, II, 21-24.
[81] *Niles' Register*, June 12, 1813.
[82] *Salem Gazette*, June 8, 11, 1813, "Answers of the Senate and the House of Representatives."
[83] *Niles' Register*, June 19, 1813.
[84] *Salem Gazette*, June 29, 1813; *Annals of Congress*, 13th, 1st, 333-41; Quincy, *Life of Quincy*, 323-24.

suggested that the state Senate adopt a resolution expressing admiration for the conduct of Lawrence, that body
dissented and, instead, resolved that in a war "waged
without justifiable cause," it was "not becoming a moral
and religious people to express any approbation of military and naval exploits" not concerned with the defense
of the state.[85] Interestingly enough, this resolution was
being considered at the very time when Lawrence in the
Chesapeake was fighting his unfortunate battle with the
Shannon, and was adopted when it was known that he had
been defeated and probably killed. Secretly the Massachusetts Federalists rejoiced at this victory of British
arms, and when the bodies of the dead captain and his
first officer were brought back from Halifax by Captain
George Crowninshield under a flag of truce, the Federalists refused to take any part in the elaborate funeral ceremonies which were arranged. In Salem, the influence of
the Pickering party, led by Samuel Putnam, was sufficient
to secure the refusal of the North Meeting House for the
ceremonies, and a third of the members of the East India
Marine Society voted against attendance.[86]

Although Pickering had approved Quincy's proposal in
regard to Louisiana and other new states from the west,
he found that the Remonstrance and other acts of the
Massachusetts Legislature were too mild for his purposes.
At Washington he found that the war party was in full
control, and he believed that it had no intention of making
peace, although Madison had already agreed to accept the
Russian offer of mediation.[87] Upon receipt of the Massachusetts Remonstrance and resolutions, he wrote to
Quincy:

"I consider the thing as utterly hopeless. More States
will be created, rather than the first disfranchised. The first
and only remedy will be when the Southern Atlantic States
shall open their eyes, and see their true interests in a firm
and close connection with the Northern half of the Union.
Then Congress will *equalize the public burdens;* and then
the Western States with Louisiana will fly off. They will

[85] *Niles' Register,* July 3, 1813.
[86] Bentley, *Diary,* IV, 191-92.
[87] Pickering MSS., Pickering to James Robertson, May 23, 1813.

detach themselves, take to their own use all the Western lands, and leave the whole national debt on the shoulders of the Atlantic States." [88]

Believing this, Pickering did not attempt to present the resolutions on the admission of new states, but confined himself to submitting the Remonstrance to Congress. [89]

Pickering's opinion of the expediency of these measures was borne out by the action of the House on the Massachusetts Remonstrance. The most that he could obtain for it was an order to have it printed, and that was secured only after an attempt of the western members to delete the charge that the admission of Louisiana had been unconstitutional. [90] At the same time, the Remonstrance was partially nullified by the protest of the minority of the Massachusetts House of Representatives, which was likewise read into the record. [91] Finally, Congress disposed of the Remonstrance by postponing action on it until the next session, [92] when it was intentionally forgotten.

The failure of the protests of 1813 served only to convince Pickering that the Federalists were taking too moderate a course. He described it later as having "just enough spirit to make it the jest of the majority," and wrote:

"Massachusetts had now become an object of contempt. The majority men and their partisans abroad concluded that Massachusetts had neither the talents nor the fortitude to plan and execute any efficient measure to check or control their destroying projects. I almost dreaded to hear of any movement in Massachusetts lest like all the former ones it should end in smoke and sink the nation deeper in disgrace." [93]

The affair confirmed the opinion that he had written to Quincy, that the only safety for the commercial states

[88] Quincy, Life of Quincy, 323-24, Pickering to Quincy, June 19,1813.   Pickering also told John Lowell (Pickering MSS., Pickering to Lowell, June 26, 1813) that it was useless to attempt the repeal of the act admitting Louisiana.

[89] Annals of Congress, 13th, 1st, 333-49.

[90] Ibid.

[91] Ibid., 350-51.

[92] Ibid., 403-05.

[93] Adams, New England Federalism, 404-06, Pickering to Lowell, Nov. 7, 1814.

lay in casting off the West and reorganizing the Union of the "good old thirteen states." He believed that the southern Atlantic states would benefit from this change as much as the North, and that if they "should ever open their eyes to see their real interest" they would willingly co-operate to bring it about. He was so certain of the correctness of this view that he predicted that such a development would necessarily take place in the future, perhaps within his own lifetime. In a letter to George Logan, to whom he confidentially expressed these ideas, he remarked that he thought that immediate separation would be a "real blessing" for the original states of the Union and asked him to consider the matter carefully.[94]

The letters to Quincy and Logan mark the point at which Pickering again became a believer in disunion as the only defense for an economic-political group that had become a permanent minority in the nation. From the time when the war measures were first undertaken in the winter of 1811-12 until the summer of 1813, he had hoped that the concerted opposition of the commercial states might defeat the administration and stop the war. But all such measures had failed. From this point on, his attitude was that the nation must choose between disunion and making concessions to the commercial states that would safeguard their interests. But for the present there was no opportunity of accomplishing either. Only a great national crisis could provide that opportunity, and for that he must wait.

In the meantime he conceived it to be his task to bend all his efforts to keeping alive the opposition to the administration. In Congress he could do little, and he seldom spoke on the questions before the House. Only once during the sessions of the Thirteenth Congress did he make an extended speech, which, incidentally, had but little to do with the subject before the House. His real purpose was to give further publicity to his view of the war, rather than to defeat the loan bill then being discussed.[95]

During the summer of 1813 he was busily engaged in

94 Adams, *New England Federalism*, 391, Pickering to Logan, July 4, 1813.
95 *Annals of Congress*, 13th, 2nd, 1697-1750.

preparing another press attack on the administration. This time his subject was the mediation of Russia. He had been sceptical of it from the beginning and he believed it to be only an administration trick to throw the blame for the continuance of the war upon Great Britain. At first he declared that the mediation suggested by Daschkoff, the Russian minister, had not been authorized by his government.[96] Madison, he thought, had accepted Daschkoff's offer in order to convince a war-weary nation that he was anxious for peace. If England should reject the proposed mediation, as Pickering was sure it would, Madison would be the gainer, as he could turn the refusal into an instrument for stirring up resentment against the British and winning support for a more vigorous prosecution of the war.[97] Perhaps, too, Pickering feared that the mediation might lead to peace without the crisis which he and his fellow-partisans hoped might be the means of restoring Federalist and New England influence in the United States.

Before actually deciding to publish his letters on the Russian mediation, Pickering learned that Daschkoff's offer was official,[98] and that information caused him to wait. For a time he seemed to believe that a peace mission under Russian auspices might bring about an acceptable treaty, for James A. Bayard, the only Federalist member of the mission, had said that his instructions were broad enough to permit the negotiation of a satisfactory peace. Pickering believed, too, that for the moment the administration was willing to make some sacrifices to secure peace rather than court the almost certain disaster which the continuance of the war would entail.[99] But a few weeks more saw him change his opinion again, as he was told by Richard Söderstrom, the Swedish Consul-General, that Daschkoff's offer was unauthorized.[100] Without further confirmation, and in spite of the disapproval

---

[96] Pickering MSS., Pickering to James Robertson, May 28, 1813.
[97] *Ibid.*, Pickering to Logan, May 26, 1813.
[98] *Ibid.*, Pickering to John Lowell, June 26, 1813.
[99] *Ibid.*, Pickering to Joseph Lewis, July 6, 1813.
[100] *Ibid*, Söderstrom to Pickering, Aug. 19, Sept. 1, 1813; Pickering to Söderstrom, Aug. 27, 1813.

of George Cabot and Timothy Williams,[101] he hastened to prepare eight articles, in which his criticism of the peace mission relied largely on the alleged unofficial nature of the mediation proposal.[102] When Söderstrom protested against such a use of a confidential opinion,[103] Pickering replied that he should feel "rather honored than injured" by the ill-will of the administration.[104]

These articles provided Pickering with another opportunity to place before the public his peculiar ideas on the war and foreign relations. In addition to his claim that Daschkoff's proposal was unauthorized, he declared, in his examination of Madison's acceptance of the offer, that although the President desired peace, he wished the negotiation to come in such a manner that he might take advantage of it if it failed. He repeated Bayard's opinion that the instructions to the peace commissioners were broad enough to admit of a satisfactory treaty and from that he inferred that the government had changed its stand on impressment. If Madison were willing simply to ask that Great Britain forbear to exercise the right of impressment, while the United States agreed to do all in its power to prevent the employment of British sailors on American vessels, Pickering was certain that peace could be arranged. The only reason for the failure of the pre-war negotiations, he said, was the insistence of Jefferson and Madison on the surrender of the right of impressment. After this analysis of the peace proposals, Pickering again called on the Federalists to refuse to support the war in any way. "Let federalists universally withhold their money and the war must soon come to an end," he wrote, and told his readers that Madison would continue to work for peace only if forced to do so.[105]

On this occasion the appeal to the people fell wide of the mark. The autumn of 1813 found New England still in that state of indecision which had characterized it from

[101] Pickering MSS., Williams to Pickering, Sept. 2, 1813.

[102] *Ibid.*, Clippings from the *Daily Advertiser*, Sept. 22, 1813, et seq.

[103] *Ibid.*, Söderstrom to Pickering, Sept. 29, 1813.

[104] *Ibid.*, Pickering to Söderstrom, Oct. 10, 1813.

[105] *Ibid.*, Clippings from the *Daily Advertiser*, Sept. 22, 1813, et seq.. "Letters on the Russian Mediation."

the beginning of the war.   More than any other section, it had prospered in war-time and, while that prosperity continued, it could not be brought to that point of resistance which Pickering desired.   Disapproval of the war and the conduct of the government were not of themselves enough to produce stronger measures.

The administration, however, soon provided the reason for a more vigorous protest.   In December, Congress passed an embargo act, designed chiefly to put an end to New England's illicit trading with the enemy.   Nothing could have produced a greater reaction against the government and the war than this, for it struck directly at the profits of the merchants who enjoyed the illegal trade with Canada, and ran directly contrary to the ingrained principles of a commercial section.

The Republican minority in New England hailed the law with delight and doubtless echoed the sentiments of "An Old Farmer," who wrote:

"Nothing ever gave me more pleasure than the Embargo Law, because I love to see a rogue tied hand and foot.   The President's message . . . does not develop a thousandth part of the villainy which was every day coming to light, in pursuance of a system of illicit trade with the enemy." [106]

But the Federalists looked at the law differently.   Governor Strong told the Legislature that its constitutionality was doubtful, and suggested the propriety of measures to force its repeal or amendment.[107]   Both the House and the Senate responded favorably.   Said the House of Representatives:

". . . we are under a solemn conviction that the time has arrived, in which it is incumbent on the people of this State to decide whether their burdens are not too grievous to be borne; and to prepare themselves for the great duty of protecting by their own vigour, their inalienable rights, and of securing for themselves at least, the poor privilege of mutual intercourse by water as well as by land." [108]

Even before the Governor and the Legislature began

[106] *Salem Register*, Jan. 5, 1814.
[107] *Salem Gazette*, Jan. 18, 1814.
[108] *Ibid.*, Jan. 25, 1814.

their discussions, the town meetings were in action. Throughout January and February they were busily petitioning the General Court to protect them from the measures of the federal government. The scenes of 1809 and 1812 were re-enacted, but the tone of the resolutions and petitions was more determined than before. Typical of the memorials emanating from the town meetings was that of the town of Belfast. Declaring that it would not again petition the general government, it avowed its intention of defending itself and announced that it would henceforth "look to the State legislature as the ark of [its] political safety." Condemning every action of the national administration, it expressed its contempt for the "tory doctrine of non-resistance and passive obedience" as it called on the Legislature for firm measures and suggested the use of the militia in resisting the orders of the national government.[109] By the middle of February, the General Court had received petitions from thirty-five legal town meetings and three other bodies.[110] Nearly all the resolutions were as militant as those of Belfast and indicated that the time was ripe for the radical measures long desired by the extremists.

At the time of these petitions Pickering was in Washington, but reports of them could not fail to reach his ears. To him they seemed to be the opportunity for which he had been waiting. At once he undertook to advise and direct the Massachusetts Legislature in its measures of resistance. Writing on February 4 to Samuel Putnam, who may be described as his personal representative in the General Court, he warned the Legislature that

"The time is arrived when *ordinary opposition* will prove futile. God forbid that there should be any more *supplications* or simple remonstrances."

At the same time he submitted a program of action. First, he suggested a statement "in strong language" of

[109] *Salem Gazette*, Feb. 18, 1814.
[110] *Ibid.*, Mar. 1, 1814. The report of the joint committee of the Senate and the House, Feb. 22, 1814, mentions petitions from thirty-five towns, "from sundry inhabitants of Plymouth and Penobscot," and from "the fishermen of Boston." The list of towns represents all parts of the state.

the "numerous violations of the Constitution and the various acts of national oppression," followed by a list of measures which would safeguard the position of the commercial states in the Union.   Second, he would

"send forth a solemn and earnest address . . . in plain, but forceful language, stating concisely all the great evils wantonly brought on . . . by the acts of the national government, and for no possible cause but to co-operate with Europe's execrable tyrant, the ruler of France."

This declaration should also list the demands for relief and point out that while it was their sincere desire to maintain the Union, past experience had demonstrated that little was to be expected from the national administration and that the people of New England must rely on themselves.   Such an appeal, he believed, would settle the question forever, especially if the governments of the other New England states would join in the protest.   Next, he urged that Massachusetts propose a New England convention to perfect measures of resistance and determine the final course of action.   Finally, he recommended that the people be encouraged to persevere in their opposition to service in the army and navy, and in their refusal to subscribe to the war loans.[111]

Three days later he wrote Putnam a second letter, indicating that he had some doubts of the wisdom of his recommendations, and that even in his own mind he was uncertain of the best policy for Massachusetts.   He explained that he was not looking to the state "for any other than preparatory measures," and hoped that his letter of the fourth did not seem to go beyond that purpose.   Yet, after giving this interpretation to his proposals and again reviewing the policies of Madison, he wrote:

". . . let me conclude with the hope and confidence, that the tones of Masachusetts will be strong and imposing; and that she will prepare to execute, boldly & firmly, the measures which a just & reasonable redress of her great and multiplied wrongs authorize and urge her to take, and in which the ardent wishes & blessings of all the good & patriotic citizens of the U. S. will attend you.   And let me once more assure

[111] Adams, *New England Federalism*, 391-93.

you that to New England, especially to Massachusetts at its head, all such men look for redemption. Let their past glory as well as her own and the general safety, animate her in the honorable attempt, which well conducted, cannot fail of success." [112]

But Pickering's advice was still to radical for many of the Massachusetts Federalists. The Boston group, which was still influential, was not yet convinced of the wisdom of his recommendations. It was notable that Boston was not among the towns which sent vigorous memorials to the Legislature. The strength of the protest movement seemed to lie in the country towns and the smaller seaports. Manasseh Cutler reported that Pickering's own county of Essex was loud in its demands for measures of relief. For himself, he believed that the secession of New England was the only remedy.[113] Putnam, in answering Pickering's letters, informed him that the committees from each county were considering courses of resistance, but expressed the fear of the radicals that the leadership of Boston would be disastrous to their program.[114]

Putnam's fears were well grounded, for the petitions of the towns were referred to a joint committee, of which James Lloyd, a moderate Boston Federalist and Pickering's former colleague in the Senate, was chairman. This committee rejected the radical program and contented itself with recommending resolutions declaring the embargo and its supplementary enforcing acts unconstitutional and instructing the Governor to lay the town memorials before the Legislature again at the June session. Taking up the modes of resistance suggested by the towns, the committee gave its opinion that a remonstrance to Congress was useless, but it would not recommend that the Legislature pass laws to protect the citizens against the war legislation of

[112] Pickering MSS., Feb. 7, 1814; printed in part in Lodge, *Cabot*, 532.

[113] *Ibid.*, Cutler to Pickering, Feb. 11, 1814, "Is not ye voice of the N. England States lost in ye national counsels? Is not ye power of the government transferred to ye south and west? And are they not able to hold it? Were our commerce to be again permitted, will it not be so burdened & cramped as to be little better than embargo?"

[114] Lodge, *Cabot*, 532-33, Putnam to Pickering, Feb. 11, 1814.

the national government. On the question of a New England convention, it declared that there was no doubt of the right of the state to call such a convention, but that it was inexpedient to do so at that time. On February 22, the Legislature adopted this report.[115]

The spring elections proved that the moderates had read the temper of Massachusetts more correctly than Pickering and Putnam. Much as they disliked the war and the embargo, the people still hesitated to take a course involving the threat of disunion. Although Caleb Strong was re-elected and Federalist majorities were again returned to the Legislature, the Republicans won a substantial increase in their vote.[116] A more extreme Federalist program might have sent many more voters into the ranks of Republicanism.

In April, Congress repealed the embargo and the course of Massachusetts seemed to be justified. When the Legislature assembled in May, Governor Strong spoke of the repeal in terms of triumph and expressed satisfaction that no measures had been taken against the federal government.[117] The Legislature agreed with his opinions and the session passed without further discussion of anti-war legislation and a new England Convention.[118]

Before the end of the summer, however, the situation had changed again and conditions seemed auspicious for a new initiation of the radical program. For the first time the war was carried directly to New England as the British established a blockade of the coast and actually occupied eastern Maine. The entire section was threatened and it was feared that Boston would be attacked. At no time during the war had the national government been so low as in the summer and early fall of 1814. Unable even to protect Washington, it could do little for

115 Ames, *State Documents*, II, 25-31.

116 *Salem Gazette*, May 31, 1814. Dexter, the Republican candidate, received 45,953 votes as compared with 42,789 for Varnum in 1813. Dexter's campaign was based largely on an appeal not to carry the opposition to the war to unconstitutional lengths and not on a plea for active support of the President. His moderation was an undoubted aid to the Republican cause.

117 *Ibid*., June 3, 1814.

118 Morrison, *Otis*, II, quoting *Mass. Resolves, 1812-1815*, 483-97.

New England. But it was not merely a question of ability. Angered by Massachusetts' persistent refusal to allow her militia to enter the national service, the War Department now refused to maintain the state troops employed in the defense of New England unless they were placed under its direction. As Strong would not agree to this, Massachusetts was left to provide men and money for her own defence.

Yet, with the British at their very door, the Massachusetts Federalists were far more interested in the discussion of opposition to Madison than in measures of defence against the national enemy. Finally, the militia were called out and in September a "Board of Commissioners for Sea Coast Defence" was organized.[119] Among the members was Pickering, but, after a few days' service, he departed for Washington, leaving a memorandum of his recommendations in the hands of the Governor. Outside of a few routine matters, his most important suggestion was that the state take over the *Constitution* and the *Independence,* then at Charlestown, if the President would not order them to assist in the defence of Boston.[120]

For the high Federalists, the British invasion at a moment of national weakness was an opportunity. The refusal of the government to defend New England seemed proof of the assertion that the administration had permanently abandoned the commercial states. Under these circumstances, Governor Strong issued a call for a special session of the Legislature to meet on October 5, 1814.[121] How far the program of action had been decided in advance is impossible to determine, but there can be little doubt that the leaders had agreed upon its major features. Practically every detail of the action taken at the special session had been discussed time and again since the first suggestion of the united opposition of New England in 1804. When the Legislature assembled, events moved without a hitch. This could scarcely have been the case unless the leaders had already perfected their plans.

[119] *Salem Gazette*, Sept. 23, 1814.
[120] Pickering MSS., Pickering to Strong, Sept. 13, 1814.
[121] Theodore Dwight, *History of the Hartford Convention* (New York, 1833), 338.

Pickering's role in the formation of plans at this time cannot be determined with any accuracy, but circumstances suggest that he must have been one of those engaged in drawing up the plans for a New England Convention and in suggesting the measures it should sponsor. He was more intimately connected with this form of protest than any other Federalist leader. He had proposed it first in 1804; suggested it again in 1809 as a means of defeating the Embargo; and had urged its adoption on two previous occasions during the war, at the Essex County Convention in July, 1812, and at the time of the protest against the war embargo in February, 1814. In September, when Strong issued the call for a special session of the Legislature, he was in Boston as a member of the "Board of Commissioners for Sea Coast Defense." Considering his attachment to the project, it can scarcely be doubted that he took every opportunity to urge it on Strong and the Federalist leaders of the Legislature. Furthermore, after going to Washington, he wrote a number of letters to influential Federalists in which he advocated that New England take a firm stand and attempted to outline a program for the Convention.[122] It is not likely that these letters, written after the plan for a convention had been set in motion, were his only contributions. They must have been preceded by conversations in Boston in which essentially the same ideas were expressed.

Substantially what had happened during the summer of 1814 was that the moderate Federalists of Massachusetts, who had succeeded in postponing the convention in February, had come to accept the proposals of the radicals as a result of the new dangers which threatened New England. When the Legislature assembled, events moved quickly to their conclusion, as the Senate and House adopted the Governor's recommendation and issued a call for a New England Convention to meet at Hartford in December. Within a few weeks more, plans were completed, for Connecticut and Rhode Island agreed to take

[122] Adams, *New England Federalism*, 394-98, 400-10, 414-18; Pickering to Strong, Oct. 12; to Morris, Oct. 21; to Lowell, Nov. 7, 28; to Hillhouse, Dec. 16, 1814.

part, while three counties in New Hampshire and Vermont expressed their willlingness to send delegates.[123]

As Pickering was not a member of the Hartford Convention, it is unnecessary to review in detail the proceedings of that body,[124] but important to note his connection with them. From the beginning he was most interested in it and looked to it for the revival not only of the influence of New England, but also the Federalist party throughout the United States.[125] His greatest fear was that its decisions would be too moderate.

"I pray God," he wrote to Caleb Strong, "that New England may not be wanting to herself and to her brethren, the most valuable members of our great political society. The dominant party have brought the United States to the brink of ruin, and treated us not as equals, but as their field laborers. . . . I am weary and indignant at this servitude, and unwilling longer to submit to it. Yet without some extraordinary effort, some act becoming the high spirit of freemen, . . . I see not but our chains are to be riveted forever." [126]

To John Lowell, he declared, "I hope the delegates of Massachusetts may now prove their readiness to *act* as well as to *speak.*" [127] At every opportunity he tried to arouse the Convention to "wise sentiments and efficient plans" that would "insure the wished-for success." [128] He did not, however, correspond directly with any delegate to the Convention except James Hillhouse. Instead, he wrote frequently to John Lowell, who, as the mouthpiece and pamphleteer of the "Essex Junto," was in a position to influence the work of the Convention.[129]

Between the time of the call for the special session of the Massachusetts Legislature and the convening of the

[123] Dwight, *History of the Hartford Convention*, 342-52; Ames, *State Documents*, II, 35-38.

[124] The best detailed account of the Convention is in Morison, *Otis*, II.

[125] Adams, *New England Federalism*, 394-98, 414-18; Pickering to Strong, Oct. 12; to Hillhouse, Dec. 16, 1814.

[126] *Ibid.*, 394-98.

[127] *Ibid.*, 404-06, Nov. 7, 1814.

[128] *Ibid.*, 404-06.

[129] *Ibid.*, 404-10.

delegates at Hartford, new measures of the administration further provoked Pickering and his friends. The desperate condition of the national finances and the army had led the President and Congress into the discussion of new taxes, paper money, and conscription. As Massachusetts was at the moment preparing to raise and finance military forces for its own defence, Pickering looked upon the proposed bills as engines of tyranny. The Conscription Bill he styled "violent and outrageous." [130] As a defence against the taxing measures, he suggested that the state governments should confiscate as much of the federal tax as necessary to pay the expenses of the militia,[131] and that Federalists should make their submission to taxation conditional on a change of administration.[132]

His anger at the administration was also increased by the attitude which it took in the peace negotiations. When the terms offered by Great Britain were learned in America, he expressed surprise that they were so mild. He had expected the British to ask for an indemnity, but found that they had asked only for security. The recognition of the right of impressment, the creation of an Indian buffer state in the Northwest, British control of the Great Lakes, and the cession of northeastern Maine in return for the continuance of the fishing privileges, were conditions of peace which any reasonable American ought to admit, he thought. In a letter to Caleb Strong he presented these conclusions with an analysis of the question of peace. Strong was so pleased with these views that he gave the letter to the press, which published it anonymously as a "letter from a gentleman of great information and enlightened Patriotism, now in Washington." [133] A few days later, another "Letter on the Negotiation at Ghent, . . . written by a distinguished member of Congress," appeared in the Federalist papers.[134] The

[130] Pickering MSS., Pickering to S. P. Gardner, Nov. 9, 1814.
[131] Adams, *New England Federalism*, 394-98.
[132] *Ibid.*, 400-02, Pickering to Morris, Oct. 21, 1814.
[133] *Columbian Centinel*, Oct. 26, 1814. This letter is also published in Adams, *New England Federalism*, 394-98, with a confidential paragraph not in the newspaper copy.
[134] Pickering MSS., newspaper clipping.

purpose of this letter, as of the first one, was to maintain the argument that the stand of the administration was unreasonable and to present an alternative peace program acceptable to Federalists, who earnestly wished that Madison might be forced to accept such unfavorable terms as these.

With the preparations for the Hartford Convention completed and with the high Federalists' ideas on peace before the public, the fall election was held. The result demonstrated that Federalist control of New England was more complete than at any previous time during the war. If the people had wished to repudiate the Federalist extremists, the election was their opportunity. However, there was every indication that the majority approved the radical program, for of the forty-one representatives from New England, the Federalists succeeded in electing all but two.[135] Pickering, whose policies were surely well known in his own district, was sent back to Congress with only a few scattered votes against him.[136]

Although Pickering had been in Washington since early fall, his real interest lay in the developments in New England. From Washington he wrote to his friends to urge the adoption of a firm stand against the administration and to recommend measures for the Hartford Convention. He approved the choice of George Cabot as head of the Massachusetts delegation, but feared that Cabot's scepticism and indifference might be a source of weakness. Such an attitude struck no responsive chord in the mind of the fanatical Pickering. "In this wicked world," he wrote, "it is the *duty* of every good man, though he cannot restore it to *innocence,* to strive to prevent its growing worse." [137] His fears were confirmed by John Lowell, who described all the Massachusetts delegates except Timothey Bigelow as too timid and conservative to take the steps which the situation demanded. Lowell believed that

[135] Adams, *History of the United States*, VIII, 228.
[136] *Salem Gazette*, Nov. 11, 1814. This time Pickering was elected from the Essex South District, as the Federalists had revised the districts in order to correct the "Gerrymander."
[137] Adams, *New England Federalism*, 406-07, Pickering to Lowell, Nov. 7, 1814.

New England must present its demands and say, "We go on no longer with you unless you agree to these stipulations." [138] It was his opinion that the rest of the nation would yield rather than face disunion. With that judgment Pickering was in substantial agreement. Before this he had written to Gouverneur Morris:

"Union is the talisman of the dominant party, and many Federalists are enchanted by its magic sound, are alarmed at every appearance of opposition to the measures of the *faction* lest it should endanger the 'Union.' I have never entertained such fears. On the contrary . . . I have said, 'Let the ship run aground. The shock will throw the pilots overboard and other competent navigators will get her once more afloat and conduct her safely into port.' I have even gone so far as to say that the separation of the Northern section of States would be ultimately advantageous, because it would be temporary and because in the interval the rights of the states would be recovered and secured, that the Southern States would earnestly seek reunion when the rights of both would be defined and established on more equal and therefore more durable bases." [139]

It is clear, then, that Pickering wished New England to secede unless it could dictate its own terms of remaining in the Union. The great danger to the interests of his native section lay in the influence of the new western states. If that influence could be eliminated, he felt that the original Union could be reconstituted on satisfactory terms. To that end he desired the Hartford Convention to propose the secession of New England or to suggest such conditions as would nullify the influence of the West. That had been his opinion in the summer of 1813, and had been expressed in his correspondence with Josiah Quincy and George Logan.[140] As time had gone on, he had become further convinced of the correctness of this idea. However, just before the Convention met, he came to the conclusion that secession was inevitable, whether initiated

[138] Adams. *New England Federalism*, 410-14, Lowell to Pickering, Dec. 3, 1814.
[139] *Ibid.*, 400-02, Pickering to Morris, Oct. 21, 1814.
[140] *Ibid.*, 391, Pickering to Logan, July 4, 1813; Quincy, *Life of Quincy*, 323-24, Pickering to Quincy, June 19, 1813.

by New England or not, for the British army was approaching New Orleans and seemed to have excellent prospects of taking it. That event could mean only one thing, the destruction of the Union, and he wrote to James Hillhouse, "From the moment that the British possess New Orleans, the union is severed." He went on to describe what he believed would be the results of the fall of the city. Louisiana would become a British province, while the trans-Alleghany states would find it expedient to set up for themselves, since the transfer of New Orleans would remove their one real bond of union with the Atlantic states. This dissolution of the United States would "annihilate the war debt" and thus leave the East burdened only with the remainder of the Revolutionary obligations. As for the South, it would find itself forced to unite with the North on northern terms. Under such conditions, the reorganization of the original union on principles acceptable to Federalists would be simple.[141]

Fantastic as this view may seem to later generations, it was the logical outcome of his extreme beliefs. His narrow sectionalism, his failure to understand the growth of national sentiment, his interpretation of national welfare in terms of the prosperity of maritime commerce, his antipathy for the frontier West, and his belief in an aristocratic government, made it impossible for him to think that the interests of New England and the principles of good government could be safe un'ess the Union were reorganized and the Constitution revised. This opinion, as well as his British sympathies, made him wish for the defeat of the Americans at New Orleans and hope for the failure of the American peace program at Ghent, since those events would aid materially in the accomplishment of his purpose.[142]

Pickering also undertook to suggest definite measures for the Hartford Convention. After urging the adoption

[141] Adams, *New England Federalism*, 414-18, Pickering to Hillhouse, Dec. 16, 1814. Similar opinions may be found in *Ibid.*, 419-20; Pickering to Samuel Hodgdon, Dec. 25, 1814; and in Pickering MSS., Pickering to Manasseh Cutler, Jan. 9; to Robert Beverley, Jan. 12, 1815.

[142] Adams, *New England Federalism*, 425, Pickering to John Lowell, Jan. 24, 1815.

of a stern course and remarking that there were "evils more to be deprecated than separation," he submitted to John Lowell a series of propositions that the Convention should sponsor as constitutional amendments to protect New England interests. These proposals were: (1) to abolish the clause permitting the counting of three-fifths of the slaves in determining Congressional representation; (2) to prohibit the interruption of commerce without the consent of nine Atlantic states; (3) to make the President ineligible for a second term; (4) to prohibit the election of a President from the same state as his predecessor; (5) to restore the original method of electing the President and Vice-President in order "to prevent the election of a fool for the latter"; (6) to reduce the appointing power of the President; (7) to make naturalization more difficult and to exclude naturalized persons from Congress and national offices; (8) to place an absolute limit on the number of representatives from new states; (9) to require a two-thirds or three-fourths vote of Congress for a declaration of war; (10) to prohibit the borrowing of money in war-time at a rate higher than the average of the year before the war in the three states contributing the largest sums to the national treasury.[143] His attitude in offering these suggestions made it clear that he would present them to the federal government as an alternative to separation.

It is not to be supposed, of course, that these proposals were Pickering's peculiar property, for anyone believing in his brand of Federalism would have favored practically the same remedies. Yet they may be taken as summarizing his program for the correction of the "evils" of the Republican government. Of his proposals, only the fifth, sixth, eighth, and tenth were not adopted by the Convention practically in the form which he had recommended to Lowell. In addition, the Convention adopted the principal of his eighth proposal when it sought to limit the powers of the western states by making the admission of new commonwealths dependent on the consent of two-thirds of both houses of Congress.[144]

[143] Adams, *New England Federalism*, 407-10, Pickering to Lowell, Nov. 28, 1814.
[144] Ames, *State Documents*, II 39-42.

However, the manner in which the Convention presented its resolutions was scarcely as bold as Pickering
would have liked. Nevertheless, he announced that he was
satisfied with the result.[145] His willingness to accept the
conclusions of a convention in which moderates like Cabot
had succeeded in avoiding the adoption of a radical program was doubtless due to the fact that he was still ex-
pecting the capture of New Orleans to make disunion
inevitable.

But all his hopes failed. In February came word that
the British had been defeated at New Orleans and that
the Treaty of Ghent had been signed. Both events con-
tributed to increase the popularity of the administration
and to discredit the Federalist opposition. As the entire
country rejoiced at the news of peace, the embassy sent
to Washington by the Hartford Convention became ridiculous,[146] and nine states summarily rejected the proposed
amendments.[147] From then on there could be no chance
of success for the New England extremists.

Pickering's whole attitude toward the War of 1812 was
marked by the same principles that had guided his career
since the time he had first become a significant political
figure. His devotion to these principles made him the
acknowledged leader of the most violent opposition to
"Mr. Madison's War." In striving to make this opposition effective, he did not hesitate to adopt any weapon
that promised success. He conceived it to be his duty
to bring defeat and disgrace on the nation in order to
discredit the administration and force it to yield to the
Federalist demands. From the beginning, he denounced
the war as unjust and urged New England to resist every
war measure. In an effort to stop the conflict, he assisted
in arousing town meetings, county conventions, and state
legislatures to bold declarations of resistance. He revived
his earlier project of a New England Convention and consistently advocated it throughout the war. Twice elected
to Congress as a pronounced opponent of the war, he was

145 Adams, *New England Federalism*, 423-25, Pickering to
Lowell, Jan. 23, 1815.
146 Morison, *Otis*, II, 167.
147 Ames, *State Documents*, II, 42-44.

constantly gaining in popularity, and at the end of 1814 he believed that he was in a fair way to see the reorganization of the Union according to the principles which he had always advocated.   But as the crisis passed and peace returned to the nation, he saw his opportunities fade as they had before.   His hope of restoring the fortunes of Federalism and of rising to power as the leader of the party had gone forever.